the trail of
TED BUNDY

Digging Up the Untold Stories

KEVIN SULLIVAN
Author of The Bundy Murders

WILDBLUE
PRESS

WildBluePress.com

Cover photograph Courtesy of the Salt Lake Tribune

The Trail of Ted Bundy published by:
WILDBLUE PRESS
1153 Bergen Pkwy Ste I #114
Evergreen, Colorado 80439

978-1-942266-37-2   Trade Paperback ISBN
978-1-942266-38-9   eBook ISBN

Book Cover and Interior Formatting by Elijah Toten
www.totencreative.com

Other Books By Kevin Sullivan

The Bundy Secrets: Hidden Files on America's Worst Serial Killer
wbp.bz/bundysecrets

Kentucky Bloodbath
wbp.bz/kb

VAMPIRE: The Richard Chase Murders
wbp.bz/vampire

For the Victims
Both the Living and the Dead

CONTENTS

PREFACE

In 2009, my book *The Bundy Murders: A Comprehensive History* was published by McFarland & Company. It's an in-depth biography of the infamous serial sex killer Ted Bundy. Published 20 years after Bundy was put to death, it was the first biography of the killer to be published in many years. The book contains new information about the case, sheds new light on a number of the murders, and it continues to be well received by those fascinated by Bundy's reign of terror.

Bundy, who became a successful killer through meticulous planning and execution of his crimes, operated in at least seven states, and during his years of murder – 1974 through most of 1975, and then again in 1978--managed to kill more than 30 women. Indeed, that number may be higher, and may in fact exceed 50, as there were murders Bundy refused to talk about. His victims were mostly young women, but he murdered teenage and preteen girls as well, and these younger victims he did not like to talk about.

Bundy's method of killing was mostly consistent, although he could deviate from his norm at any moment. Many women were whacked on the head with a crowbar, and almost all were finished off through strangulation while Bundy had sex with them from behind. Necrophilia in various forms was usually a part of the murders, too, especially if Bundy had the time to spend with them after they died or if he was able to return to the remains at a later date. This, of course, was not always possible. One of the most bizarre aspects of this sexual deviance is that while living in Washington (where the murders began), Bundy kept as many as four women's heads in his apartment at a rooming house where he was living. That he used these heads for sexual pleasure, there is little doubt.

So this retrospective look–a "back story" if you will, into the life of America's most diabolical serial killer--will not be another biography. Rather, it's a deeper look into his crimes across various states containing new and interesting information about the case; a case that to this day still has a sense of mystery surrounding it. It is, in fact, a search for additional truth and, as such, is an excellent companion volume to *The Bundy Murders*.

Within these pages you'll read new testimony from those who knew the killer, from friends of the victims, and from others who were involved in this story one way or another. Indeed, this book records for history many important voices that would otherwise go silent after the passage of time. In my view, to not add these voices to the record would be a crime.

It also includes new and previously unpublished stories from some of Bundy's Mormon friends, whom the killer met after he moved to Utah to attend law school. He sought out their friendship, proclaiming an interest in the Church of Jesus Christ of Latter-day Saints. They, of course, welcomed him with open arms, believing him to be a good and honest man. But like those who "knew" Bundy in his home state of Washington, they would later be shocked to learn of Bundy's true inner drives and intentions. Bundy's monstrous desires and cravings to kill and mutilate women were not easy for many of his friends to believe, and some would not accept that these dark accusations against him were true until the end, when Bundy finally started to come clean.

I must also note that the bulk of the testimony you'll be reading in this book (new interviews and the written record) comes from people from Washington and Utah, as these are the two states where Ted Bundy put down roots and developed relationships with many people. But I have new interviews and testimony as well from California, Oregon, Idaho, and Colorado, as well as additional material that will enlighten the reader with facts usually seen only by those conducting in-depth archival research into the Bundy case.

On top of all this I have also taken a closer look at some of the murders, their locations, and some oddities and new discoveries that weren't in the first book, and there are photographs of all of those sites. It will, without a doubt, be a most fascinating excursion into Ted Bundy and his unequaled time of terror.

A personal note: When I finished *The Bundy Murders*, at 5:21 a.m., July 17, 2008 (yes, I wrote it down), I was exhausted emotionally and physically from my 2½-year marathon into the life of Ted Bundy. By the time I typed that last word, I felt like I knew the killer better than some members of my own extended family. I also discovered along the way (and in the years since) that the victims became a part of my life. There isn't a day that goes by that I don't think about them and the man who took their lives. Not to sound overly dramatic, but it is as if the case has been indelibly printed deep within the recesses of my being, and for the rest of my life it will be there. And frankly, that's fine with me. It goes with the territory.

Once the book was published, I was more than willing to answer questions about the case, and I even knocked out the occasional article. But the thought of writing another book where the focus would be Ted Bundy? Not a chance! That was out. I couldn't imagine delving into that dark world once again. So when a writer asked me a couple of years ago to co-author a book about the killer, where we'd be exploring *possible* new aspects of the case, I politely said no. And then, in the spring of 2015, I spoke with someone closely connected to the investigation, and discovered they were having significant medical problems. Understanding that time waits for no one (it's been 41 years since Bundy began his murderous career), I knew it was time to seek out people and consult the case files one more time. We owe it to future generations to record now those voices still out there who are willing to talk.

The result of that decision is the book you're about to read.

Louisville, Kentucky
Fall 2015

CHAPTER ONE
The Washington Murders

On December 20, 1974, *Black Christmas*, a Canadian "slasher" film, was released (for perhaps a somewhat limited release) in the United States. It was based on a series of murders that occurred in Montreal, and the movie depicts the killing off – one by one – of a houseful of sorority sisters. Of course, it's unknown if Ted Bundy ever saw this film, and by Christmastime in 1974, he'd been murdering women for almost a year. But it is known that Bundy later told authorities it might behoove them to stake out theaters showing slasher films when they're looking for killers. Bundy, who knew quite a bit about avoiding detection, was no doubt on to something.

Without question, Bundy's impact on the state of Washington was the most horrific and psychologically altering reign of terror in collective memory. Beginning in January 1974 until the killer silently slipped out of the state that September, the region was subjected to the ongoing strange disappearances of college-aged women. Before he moved on to another killing ground, Bundy would murder at least eleven women, all within a span of eight months.

Some of these women became victims after Bundy tricked them into following him from public areas, while others were attacked in secluded spots. Hitchhikers who accepted a ride from him were often not seen again. In one case, he actually entered a women's rooming house while the roommates slept, attacked a coed, and carried her off into the night.

As previously mentioned, Bundy's method of killing often began with cracking victims over the head with a tire iron, rendering them unconscious. This would be followed by Bundy having intercourse with them, either vaginal or anal. For Bundy, it was all about possessing his victims: mentally, physically, metaphorically.

And as always, when a serial killer of women begins operating, the full scope of what's happening in that particular geographic area remains a mystery. It's only after a pattern of missing or murdered women begins to emerge that the authorities take notice. For Bundy, that pattern would take several months to form, as the number of missing women–women who were, almost exclusively considered low-risk for abduction and murder–began to increase in the Seattle area and throughout the state.

I covered in great detail Bundy's birth, childhood, and growth into manhood in *The Bundy Murders*, so I will refrain from repeating most of this information for this companion volume. I will, however, touch upon pertinent aspects of Bundy's life and surroundings during that time where warranted.

When Bundy was a small boy, his mother, Eleanor Louise Cowell, who had him out of wedlock in 1946 when she was 22, moved to Washington state from her parents' home in Philadelphia, marrying a man named John Bundy in 1951. The family would expand as Louise and John Bundy had four children together. In 1952 a daughter, Linda, was born, followed by a son, Glen, in 1954. The last girl to be born to the Bundy family, Sandra, entered the world in 1956. Richard, their last child, was born in 1961.

Without question, the Bundys were a normal American

family, and John and Louise Bundy were loving parents to their five children. As the years passed, all of the Bundy kids were developing well--emotionally and mentally--within this stable environment. Indeed, there was nothing intrinsic within that nucleus of seven people that could have birthed the homicidal abnormality that became Ted Bundy. Whatever it was that started the process within the child that would one day guide him into a life of unrelenting murder, began when he was but a small boy. Indeed, to find any "evidence" of the oddities within young Teddy, we must take a closer look at the first few years of his life.

When Theodore Robert Cowell was born on November 24, 1946, at a home for unwed mothers in Burlington, Vermont, he came into the world both looking and acting normal. He was no doubt cute, adorable and ready for the nurturing that Louise was more than ready to give him. But under the surface of the child, deep within his personality, there were areas of damage that Louise couldn't see, and even if she had recognized them, she'd be unable to rescue her son. In this respect, it was probably better that it was all hidden from her.

Immediately after his birth, Louise and young Teddy returned to Philadelphia to live with her parents and sisters, and all would apparently go well, despite the persistent rumors that would later surface that her father was a violent man with an easily ignited temper. Bundy would never acknowledge this, as he remembered him only as a kind and loving grandfather, and it's clear he looked up to him.

But a fracturing of Ted's personality was in fact already occurring. His aunts would later tell of the strange things Ted would do, for no apparent reason. The most striking of these was when one of them suddenly awakened and found her young nephew placing kitchen knives pointing at her underneath the covers of her bed. This alone speaks of something very amiss within the personality of the boy. And that which churned within the child was destined, in the years to come, to alter his life and the lives of many others.

And speaking of oddities: It is a fact that for a while Ted believed that his mother was his sister and his grandparents were his parents. How all of this got going remains a bit of a mystery. But contrary to some popular (but incorrect) beliefs that Bundy wouldn't learn the truth until he was grown, and perhaps this was the reason he turned into a monster, he learned the truth while still a child. In fact, there isn't anything in the record that I've discovered that pointed to this having any lasting effect on him at all. And it may very well be that this was believed by him only a short time.

However, it is an established fact that Bundy grew up to have significant problems because of his illegitimate birth. Although he was thought to most likely be the result of a brief love affair between his mother and a World War II naval veteran by the name of Jack Worthington, which would at least have given him a sense of where he came from (if indeed Louise revealed this to her son), it was never enough. It didn't matter that John Bundy adopted Ted and gave him his name, it wasn't enough. And this internal battle Bundy would carry within himself did in fact produce a rage within him. But again, this has nothing to do with the fracturing of his personality as witnessed by his family as early as his toddler years in Philadelphia.

In any event, when Ted was in the second grade, the Bundy family purchased a home at 658 N. Skyline Drive in Tacoma, not far from the Narrows Bridge. During my research for the first book I wasn't able to visit his boyhood home, or any other location in the state. All my research was conducted through the case files, photographs (both from the time and more recently), maps, etc. So it was especially important for me to be able to walk the grounds and photograph these locations, not to find out what happened there, but to get a "feel" for the area and capture the images for this book. Skyline Drive is a nice, middle-class neighborhood, and is no doubt very similar to the socioeconomic makeup as when the Bundy family lived here.

The boyhood home of Ted Bundy at 658 North Skyline Drive in Tacoma, Washington.

Standing on the street and gazing at the home provided me same view I've seen many times before on the Internet through the pictures taken by previous visitors. Wanting a bit more than the standard photo, I was determined to obtain additional shots of the home, especially of the backyard where Bundy as a small child would have played. Not wanting to appear as a trespasser, I walked up the walkway, ascended the steps and rang the doorbell. Within moments an elderly German woman answered the door, quickly followed by her middle-aged son. After introducing myself as a writer, and showing them a copy of *The Bundy Murders*, I asked for permission to photograph the rear of the home. At first they seemed a little reticent, telling me there were moving boxes and other items waiting to be picked up and loaded onto a truck. I assured them it was fine "as is" and that I just wanted a picture or two anyway. They quickly agreed, but before I turned around to leave, the son offered to let me come in and see the room they believed had belonged to Ted Bundy. I quickly said no, that it wouldn't be necessary (I thought later, "Well, that was a mistake!"), and I thanked them for giving me their okay to take photographs and proceeded to walk around to the rear of the house.

I must say, looking at the home and the back and front yards, it was easy for me to imagine Bundy as a small child playing here. It is, at least for me, very sad to contemplate such a scene, because little Teddy Bundy was, from all outward appearances, just a normal child. Those who saw him must have considered him a sweet little kid, and that's a perfectly normal reaction. No one who knew him could ever have imagined what he would become. And this is why I wrote in *The Bundy Murders*, that:

"Before Bundy ever stretched out his hand to murder his first victim, he was a victim himself, of his own internal devices. No matter how monstrous he ultimately became, the first life to be destroyed would be his own. Without the fracturing of his personality in his early years and his drifting, by degrees as it were, into the completely unfettered life of a sociopathic serial killer, the course of his life and the lives of others would have been totally different. The death of almost everything normal had to have occurred within Bundy by January of 1974. Had it not, most if not all of the women he murdered would be alive today, many with children and grandchildren. These are the unknowns, whose births and futures were voided long ago by the madman."

At about the time Ted Bundy was graduating from Wilson High School in the spring of 1965, the Bundy family sold their house on Skyline Drive and moved to another home.

As an adult, Ted Bundy's main residence in Seattle was at Ernst and Freda Rogers' rooming house at 4143 Twelfth Ave. NE. It would be there that Bundy would later tell authorities he had as many as four women's heads in his second story apartment at one time (his room was in the southwest corner of the building). There is now a fence surrounding the house, and unless you go across the street and stand on a building's steps, you can't see the entire structure. However, it's easy to photograph the upstairs apartment where Bundy lived, and I was able to take a good shot of the back and side of the house.

James Doros, a resident at the Rogers' rooming house, met Bundy in June 1974. He told King County Detective Roger Dunn during an interview in October 1975 that he liked and admired Bundy "for his lifestyle (and) the fact that he was going to law school and able to live on a nominal budget." Although Doros admitted he never socialized with Bundy outside of the rooming house, the two men did, on occasion, drink together, and he said the wine and beer made Bundy "pretty high," He also mentioned that he could become "a little rowdy" but was never a problem drunk. Although Bundy left the rooming house for good in September 1974, Doros said that he did return for three or four days in May or June 1975 to "put in a garden for the Rogers."

Marlin Vortman, a good friend of Bundy's and an attorney he knew from his Seattle days, said that he'd seen Bundy drunk a few times and that Ted "liked rum daiquiris." Vortman also told investigators that he never saw any deviant behavior out of Bundy, but that he did believe some of the things Bundy carried in his car (his murder kit) sounded like "burglar's tools."

During my research for *The Bundy Murders*, I spoke by phone with one of the residents of the Rogers' rooming house, and he too liked Bundy. But many things come back to people in retrospect, and he mentioned that one day, when he returned home, he saw Bundy standing across the street, talking with two young teenage girls he assumed to be about 13 or 14 years old. At the time he thought nothing of it. After the rooming house residents discovered their former roommate was a cold-blooded killer, it took on an entirely different meaning.

In retrospect, it was simply Washington's misfortune that Louise moved to the city of Brown's Point in that state when Teddy was four years old. Had this not occurred, the murders would have likely begun in Pennsylvania, or wherever else she might have migrated to, and branched out from there. Of course, chance being what it is, we can't know if Ted Bundy would have been as successful had his trail of murder been anywhere else. He may have been captured early on through some unforeseen mishap, or perhaps even killed. The "what if's" are endless. All we know for certain is that, like a perfect storm, Ted Bundy operated with impunity in Washington from the time the killings began until he moved to his new hunting ground in Salt Lake City, Utah.

As to the Washington murders, I will say that my primary (and official) time period for when the killings began was in the early morning hours of February 1, 1974. This is when Bundy actually launched himself into unabated murder. By January of 1974, he had mentally and emotionally waved goodbye to his dreams of becoming a lawyer or politician. He'd discarded any of the previous thoughts that perhaps he'd actually marry his girlfriend Liz Kendall, a divorced single mother, and become a good father to her daughter. All of that was now gone, a dream never to be realized.

This road of murder he was now on had no exit ramps, and Bundy knew that his only true and lasting desire was to kill young women and girls. He craved this experience like no other, and it was far too important to him to let the mask of a normal life get in the way. This life, Bundy understood, of fulfilling his homicidal desires, would continue until he was apprehended or killed.

I must mention, before we begin the list of Bundy's known victims in Washington, the possibility of him being involved in the disappearance of eight-year-old Ann Marie Burr from her Tacoma home on September 1, 1961. Indeed, I covered this case in the preface of *The Bundy Murders*. Now, there isn't any "hard" evidence linking Bundy to this abduction and murder of a little girl (Bundy was fourteen at the time and lived about two miles away), and there isn't hard evidence that exonerates him either. But in my view, one thing does inexorably link him to this case, and that's an interview Bundy had while he was imprisoned in Florida with Ron Holmes, a well-known criminologist from Louisville, Kentucky.

During the interview, the killer readily links himself to this murder while speaking (as he had done with previous writers) in the third person, and portions of this interview were published in a May 9, 1987, article in *The Tacoma News Tribune*. In that article Bundy speaks of a person "involved in a series of murders in Washington near Lake Sammamish State Park," (where Bundy would later abduct two of his victims) and goes on to explain how this person may have started killing much earlier in life, with a first victim possibly being a girl as young as eight or nine. By mentioning Lake Sammamish in this context, Ted Bundy is linking himself to the abduction and murder of Ann Marie Burr. Not only did I have this article as part of my research into this murder, but I interviewed Ron Holmes in his office in Louisville, and he reiterated to me the very same story. Again, the story has plausibility wrapped around it at every turn.

And yet, some people doubt the veracity of this "confession," and I've personally heard the detractors attempting to negate this story altogether. I found this extremely odd from the moment I encountered the controversy, but I also understood why it was happening. This was just one more incident, in a line of incidents, that I became privy to during the research into my first Bundy book. And it all boils down to the strange pet jealousies and differing opinions among *some* of the investigators and *others* closely connected to this case.

While I've never put any of these squabbles to print, I will do so now in this one instance because of the very real possibility that Ted Bundy did in fact kill little Ann Marie Burr and, if so, that what the killer told Ron Holmes is the only real look into this abduction and murder we're ever going to get. As such, this information should not be dismissed or tossed aside unless there is verifiable evidence to support such a rejection. Those I've spoken to, however, who do reject Holmes' claim have done so without any supporting evidence at all. So with this in mind, let's look at the story.

In the mid-1980s, Holmes met with Bundy at Florida State Prison near Stark, Florida. During the interview, Holmes related, a tape recorder was not used because the room was not equipped with an electrical wall outlet (see Holmes' book, *Serial Murder*, co-authored with James De Burger). According to the book, the meeting was to be an "all day interview."

During the questioning, Holmes inquired whether this person they were talking about (Bundy) could have started killing earlier in life. And this is where Bundy launched into how "this person" may have started much earlier, starting with a girl as young as eight or nine. The substance of this face-to-face meeting penned afterward by the criminologist appears both natural and reasonable, and it has that all-important "ring of truth" one looks for in such reports. However, because there isn't a voice recording of this third-person "confession," it's now being dismissed by some as fiction. This, in my opinion, is exceedingly unwise and wouldn't pass muster for any normal investigative procedure.

The argument, some have said, is that Bundy later denied having made the confession to Holmes. But this isn't unusual for Bundy, as he did admit to crimes only later to deny them. And more to the point (and especially to the point), these denials came *after* Bundy and Holmes had had a falling out, which may very well have propelled Bundy into the denial heard later by others. Indeed, when I first interviewed former King County Police Detective Bob Keppel in a 2007 phone interview, we discussed Holmes and his role with Bundy. Keppel said that Holmes was on track to becoming Bundy's "golden boy," stating that Holmes would have been the one Bundy would have confessed all of his crimes to had things not gone sour between them. And I believe Keppel is correct about this.

None of this information proves anything, of course, but it may very well be that Holmes caught Bundy at just the right moment, and a one-time-only acknowledgment came out of the killer that sheds light on those terrible early morning hours of September 1, 1961. In my previous Bundy book I use those pertinent quotes Bundy made about her disappearance, but I didn't add Holmes' comment about the logistics of the Burr abduction and murder which I now include here, taken directly from *The Tacoma News Tribune* article and published in the local section on Saturday, May 9, 1987:

"After luring the child from the house, the other person

took the child to a nearby orchard and strangled her and then probably raped her, Holmes said Bundy told him. The Burrs, who have since moved to another North End neighborhood, said a former neighbor maintained a small fruit orchard. The opened window found the day Ann Marie disappeared faced the orchard and was on 'the dark side of the house.'"

Do I believe that Ted Bundy is responsible for the abduction and murder of Ann Marie Burr? Maybe yes, maybe no. The truth of the matter is we'll probably never know what happened to her. It's been fifty-four years since the child's disappearance, and the passage of additional time will only ensure the mystery will continue. The better question would be do I believe Ted Bundy connected himself to her disappearance when he was interviewed by Ron Holmes? Yes, I absolutely do. And as far as I'm concerned, it doesn't matter what Bundy later said, or denied, about the incident after he became angry with Ron Holmes. The truth of the matter for me is that I believe he confessed to this murder two years before his own death in Florida's electric chair, to a man he expected to ultimately confess all of his crimes. And yet, the mystery continues.

In the summer of 2015, when I visited the Burr home at 3009 N. Fourteenth St. in Tacoma, I was struck by how nice the neighborhood was after all these years. Not only has it been well maintained, but it has a very inviting feel to it. Standing out in front of the house on a sunny day snapping photographs, it was inconceivable to me that something so horrible could have happened in such a nice neighborhood. And yet, it really did happen there.

And now, on to the known murders of Theodore Robert Bundy ...

The first known victim of Bundy was a young woman I referred to in my previous book as Terri Caldwell. She lived in Seattle's university district at 4325 Eighth Ave. NE, but she

THE TRAIL OF TED BUNDY

was not a student. The house where she lived in a basement apartment is now long gone, replaced by apartments. It was a little after 2:00 a.m. on January 4, 1974, when Bundy, by way of an unlocked door, entered her dwelling and bludgeoned her about the head, nearly killing her. He also rammed a medical device known as a speculum into her vagina, such was his rage at the female of the species. As he quietly slipped out the door, he believed she was either dead or soon would die. Seriously injured, Caldwell would lie in bed until the early evening hours of the next day before her male roommates discovered her unconscious in her bed. That he hadn't killed the young woman probably disturbed Bundy, and it should be noted that he never made that mistake again. All future victims would become homicides--he would see to it.

January 31, 1974, would be the last normal day for Lynda Ann Healy, 21, who was living with four other coeds in a house at 5517 Twelfth St. NE, a few blocks from Terri Caldwell's apartment. It was a Thursday, the weekend was fast approaching, and, like all busy young people, she was probably already making plans. However, no matter what thoughts were flowing through her mind that day and evening, it's unlikely the thought of her own death crossed her mind. After all, she had her whole life ahead of her.

That evening she made dinner for her housemates, and later she, two of the housemates and a friend of Lynda's by the name of Pete Neil, walked the few blocks to Dante's tavern at 5300 Roosevelt Way NE. There they enjoyed themselves, and then around 9:30 p.m. Lynda and her friends returned home. Unbeknown to them, a person had followed them home. Keeping a safe distance, Bundy probably watched them all enter the house, and he may have still been there a few minutes later when Pete Neil hurried out the front door with his record albums. He needed to hurry so he could catch the 9:41 bus back to his place.

Later (the exact time is unknown), Bundy walked up the steps of the rooming house and gently tried the front doorknob. Turning it ever so slowly, he found the door to be unlocked. No doubt feeling gratified, he slowly released the knob and quietly walked back down the steps. His plan at that exact moment was set: He would return, he determined, in the middle of the night and perform his work at that time.

So it was, then, that during the early morning hours of February 1, Ted Bundy let himself in through the unlocked door, walked down the steps to the basement, and entered the bedroom of Lynda Ann Healy. Sleeping next door (separated only by a thin wall made of plywood) was Karen Skaviem. Karen would later tell authorities that she had trouble falling asleep, but drifted off, she believed, around 1:30 a.m., and that she heard nothing unusual during the night.

Did Bundy pick out Lynda specifically to attack her or simply choose a room by chance? We don't know. What we do know is that after entering Healy's room, he choked her into unconsciousness, which gave her a nosebleed that caused the blood to run to the back of her neck, stain her nightgown, and leave a pool of red on the bed. Like a meticulous psychopath with all the time in the world, he removed her nightgown and hung it up in the closet. After gathering up some clothes and a backpack, he made the bed (unbelievable!), and then carried the unconscious young woman up the steps and out the side door.

Now, some believe Bundy must have parked his car in the alleyway behind her house. But if this is true, he took a big chance, as the alley is so narrow that to do so would effectively block it. And yet, it seems inconceivable that Bundy would have carried her out the side door, follow the walkway the few feet to the front of the house, proceed down the steep front steps, and walk to wherever his car was parked on the street--and yet he may have done exactly that.

Add to this that he abducted a young woman from a university district, where it wouldn't be unusual to see college kids walking about in the middle of the night, and you have a recipe for disaster for the killer. But be it an alleyway or the street, these risks didn't bother Ted Bundy at all. He came for a victim, and he got one.

It is of interest to note that on November 5, 1975, Detective Roger Dunn spoke by phone with a Marlis Gilbert, a student teacher assistant at the University of Washington in Seattle, where Bundy had graduated with a degree in psychology in June 1972. Investigators were wondering if Bundy and Lynda Healy had known each other, as both were taking classes in psychology at the same time. Gilbert was, the report states: "the leader of a research group that included Lynda Healy and a few other students (and that) she knew of no direct connection between Healy and Bundy." Gilbert said she'd check the records to see whether they'd had a class together. And then she said something very interesting: She told Dunn she believed she had shared a psychology class with Bundy in 1971 that pertained to deviant behavior in children. And she said that "looking at Bundy's class schedule, he had Psyche 410 at the time and it was Deviant Behavior."

Anyone today visiting the house where Lynda Ann Healy lived with her friends, as I did in 2015, will find it in a very nice neighborhood that is well maintained, perhaps better maintained now than in 1974. Standing in front of the structure, there is no obvious reminder that evil once invaded this dwelling in the middle of the night. Just off to the right of the front door, on the side of the house, is the door leading to the basement. It was through this door that Bundy would carry Lynda out into the chilly night air.

As I walked up the steps my mind was riveted on that night. I thought of Bundy, and how he also had walked up these steps before slowly turning the doorknob that cold evening to see if it was unlocked. Having already written *The Bundy Murders*, I was well aware of what transpired there, and, at such a moment, it all becomes so very real. Indeed, in my view, the Lynda Healy abduction is the strangest of the serial killer's career, and I don't ever expect to hear of one more bizarre, either from the past or in the future.

I rang the doorbell, hoping someone would be home. It was my desire to photograph the steps leading down to the basement, as it would provide the modern version of a police photo of the same steps published in my first book. Unfortunately, no one answered, and the shots of the outside of the home would have to do. Because the front door had two strips of glass running vertically on each side, I was able to peer into a part of the kitchen, and had a good view of the living room off to the left, where Lynda's housemates met with Lynda's father and brother that terrible evening. Standing on the front porch on a mild summer evening in 2015, I was struck with how surreal it was.

Lynda Ann Healy would die soon after she was carried out into the night by Ted Bundy.

If you visit the former Healy residence, take the time to check out Dante's, too, only a few blocks away. Entering the tavern is like going back in time, as it has the same ambience as it did in 1974, and to prove it they have pictures from that time period hanging on their walls. They even have on display something they call "the Bundy sofa" (he apparently used this one quite often while he lived in Seattle), which must be quite the conversation piece among regulars. It's also interesting to note that the same family has owned the tavern for the past 50 years. When I visited the establishment in the summer of 2015, the son of the original owner, along with the staff, were very helpful and answered all my questions.

Donna Manson enrolled at Evergreen State College in the fall of 1973. The nineteen-year-old was a first-year student and, regrettably, not a very good one. There were problems with attendance, some issues with illegal drug use, and overall she appeared to be having trouble gaining traction toward a productive life. She also had absolutely no idea what was coming toward her.

When Ted Bundy first set his eyes on Evergreen State College, he must have been pleased beyond words. Scanning it with a predatory eye, he would have seen the endless opportunities available for a human predator at such a place. As I wrote in my book, *The Bundy Murders*:

"Carved out of a beautiful forest of fir trees, the concrete complex known as Evergreen State College blends well into its natural surroundings. There is a definite harmony visible there between the ruggedness (and sometimes ruthlessness) of the forest, and the warmth and safety of civilization, something thing the school has managed to maintain to this very day."

Walking the campus during my 2015 trip, it was evident that little has changed at the school since that March in 1974. The trails weaving their way through the campus offer seclusion at every turn. Even without knowing what happened here, it can easily give a person the creeps if one begins to dwell upon the slasher or horror films they've seen growing up, or if they contemplate the ultimate of horrible realities: the serial killer.

Donna Manson lived in the first-year student housing that was in the northeastern part of the campus. When she walked out of her apartment on March 12, 1974, it was around 7:00 p.m. She was headed on foot by herself to a jazz concert/dance being performed by the Evergreen Jazz Ensemble on the main floor of the library that was to begin at 8:00 p.m. She left in plenty of time, and because it was drizzling and still cool, it's certain that she wouldn't have wasted any time getting inside the library and obtaining a good seat.

This is a shot from the second floor of the library at Evergreen State College. On the night Donna Manson disappeared, she was headed to this library for a jazz concert being held on the first floor. She either ran into Bundy in this outside area, or perhaps she encountered him on one of the secluded trails leading from her apartment to the library.

Although the distance between her apartment and the library was perhaps no more than 300 yards, it was impossible to see the library (or most other buildings for that matter) from the apartment, due to the thick forest separating them. Her path to the concert (there were two she could take), would be on a winding trail encased in the ever-present fir trees, and would not have taken her very long to walk. These paths converged at the library, and I took a photograph of this area from the library's second floor. It is most likely there, on the trail, that Bundy encountered Donna Manson.

Donna Manson did not make it to the library--not inside the library, anyway. Indeed, no one remembered seeing her there or on the trail leading from the first-year student housing. To all involved, it appeared she vanished into thin air, and it would be many years before partial answers would come from the one responsible for her disappearance. A report like that of her "vanishing," of course, was becoming a familiar statistic to the detectives working the mounting number of cases of missing women in the state of Washington. Such mysterious disappearances would only serve to heighten the fears of many in the affected communities, as there were no sure answers as to what had happened to the women or where they had gone.

For Ted Bundy, college libraries were the epicenter of abduction and murder. Although he made use of every opportunity to snatch young girls and women from wherever they might be, he was still a creature of habit. And for Bundy, a percentage of the murders began at his favorite hunting ground: university libraries.

Why libraries? Bundy never explained it, but it's clear he wasn't dissuaded from operating near them due to the sometimes large groups of people that would be coming and going around him. As we will see in the upcoming abduction of Susan Rancourt, even the possibility of running into a close childhood friend at a college didn't bother Bundy. In his mind, he was impervious to detection, and, for the most part, he was right. Here's what we know about Bundy and his seeking of prey at libraries: Washington (yes); Oregon (yes); California (high probability); Idaho (yes); Utah (yes); Florida (maybe). Libraries were special to Ted Bundy, and for all the wrong reasons.

So in the case of Donna Manson, he either stopped her before she entered the library (most likely she would have encountered him on the aforementioned side of the library where two of the trails meet) and led her away with a ruse, or perhaps he waylaid her on the forested trail and carried her to his car. This, of course, would depend on where his car was parked. If it were nearby, he may have attacked her and quickly done just that. Or, if he used a ruse of some type, she may have left the trail to the library and followed him to another location where he subsequently attacked her. But no matter the mechanics of this or any other abduction Bundy committed, this much is certain: His ability to escape detection would become a frustrating hallmark in all of these missing-women cases, leaving investigators scratching their heads. The only thing detectives could say with certainty was that Donna Manson was now gone.

In April of 1974, Ted Bundy left Seattle and drove east over the Cascade Mountains, as he journeyed towards Ellensburg and Central Washington State College, now known as Central Washington University. He had not come to take any classes, but to kill another young woman. Indeed, he would make this particular college a target for at least three days and perhaps as many as five.

That he chose this particular college is more than a little surprising, as one of the students attending was none other than a good boyhood friend, Terry Storwick (later, after Bundy was convicted in Utah for the kidnapping of Carol DaRonch, Storwick's mother would write a letter to the judge looking to help Ted). I don't believe there's any way Bundy could have been unaware that his friend was attending CWSC then. Storwick could have encountered Bundy at any moment as the killer trolled about the library and surrounding buildings, fumbling with books and packages while feigning injury. Apparently, none of this mattered to Bundy, and Storwick and Bundy never crossed paths here.

Fortunately, when I was writing about Bundy's activities at CWSC for *The Bundy Murders*, I had all the case file

material, and could write the story of the abduction of
Susan Rancourt accurately. But I did have a few questions
that would never quite go away, such as, where exactly was
the "bridge" that the potential victims spoke of when they
encountered Bundy, and what was the exact location of the
train trestle Bundy parked near in a desolate no parking
zone?

The area of Bundy's hunting centered on the Bouillon
Library (now Bouillon Hall), which sits between Walnut
Street, in front, and Chestnut Street, which runs along the
rear of the library. If one stands in front of the library, Black
Hall is on the left, facing the side of the library. Squeezed in
between these two buildings was a round structure known
as the Grupe Conference Center (still standing today). In
1974, there was a small man-made pond that ran between
the conference center and Bouillon, and the bridge spoken
of in the record ran over this pond and parallel to the library.
So walking this bridge means you're either walking toward
the library or away from it, as students could only enter
the building through the main front doors. Knowing this is
critical to understanding Bundy's movements in conjunction
with one of his potential victims, and I'll have more about
this shortly.

At one time, the Milwaukee rail line angled its way
through the campus, but the railroad trestle Bundy made use
of is now long gone. I brought along for my visit a copy
of a map of this area that investigators used and on which
they had marked locations pertaining to the murder victim,
potential victims, and location of Bundy's parked car. At the
time Bundy pulled into this area, which is approximately
150-plus feet from the library (and only a slightly bit closer
to Black Hall), it was very much a desolate area. The closest
building, Black Hall (not the Black Hall of today, where
additions have been added, making it appear from the air

like an "H" shape rather than one elongated structure), was not giving off much light. And the two parking lots available to students for this area were both north and south of this location and too far away to provide sufficient illumination. Today, buildings sit all around this location, and the two parking lots have now joined to become one massive parking area, essentially gobbling up this infamous spot. So with the trestle removed and the uninhabited now habited, you must, while standing there, mentally visualize what it must have looked like as Susan Rancourt walked with Ted Bundy to his Volkswagen on that dark night of April 17, 1974.

What follows is a passage from my book describing another young woman whom Bundy tried but failed to abduct, Kathleen D'Olivo, and references the bridge Bundy used that night to lead her away to his car:

"Descending the steps leading to the first floor, Kathleen left through the front entrance, immediately turned right, stepped off the concrete patio area at the front of the building and began walking across the grassy area. She stepped back onto the sidewalk and continued walking towards Black Hall and the parking lot where her vehicle was located. Within moments of this, however, she heard the sound of something like books hitting the pavement. 'I turned around,' she would later tell police, 'and there was a man dropping books. He was squatting, trying to pick up the books and packages ... I noticed that he had a sling on one arm, and a metal hand brace on the other. I just noticed he was unable to pick up that many things and I assumed that he was going into the library.' Kathleen, approaching the situation with caution, offered to help. 'Yeah, could you?' he replied.

"'I thought he was going to the library. He was headed that way, so I thought that's where he was going. But that same sidewalk actually leads up over a little bridge [and away from the library] ... It's just a short bridge that goes over a man-made pond and [the sidewalk] ... will angle off to go into the library.'

"But instead of continuing on the pathway to Bouillon Library, the disabled man started across the bridge. This threw up a red flag for Kathleen, who instantly said: 'Wait a minute ... where are we going?' 'Oh, my car is just parked right over here,' he said, as he motioned in the direction it would be located.

"The distance to his car, once they crossed the bridge, was about 150 feet. It was conveniently parked in a secluded, dimly lighted section, on the edge of the campus in a no parking area under a railroad trestle bounded by tall grass. It was the perfect spot to commit a murder, or at least begin one. The road leading to the trestle, Kathleen said, 'was not well traveled.'"

Oddly, he did not attack Kathleen D'Olivo that day, and she would escape from the clutches of Ted Bundy. But, soon after, fellow CWSC student Susan Rancourt would not. Believing Bundy's apparent injuries to be real, like the others, she followed him to his car. This time, Bundy was able to overpower his "helper" and within a short time the killer was speeding away from the campus.

Kent Barnard, a student at Edmonds Community College in Edmonds, Washington, that spring of 1974, had driven to CWSC to spend the day with his girlfriend, Deanna Gavin. April 17 was Kent's birthday, and I'm sure he was counting on making it memorable to some degree. It would be very memorable, of course, but not in the way he originally imagined.

Recently, in a phone conversation, Barnard told me that he first passed the man with the dark sling on his arm as he stood in front of the library sometime around 2:00 p.m. What follows is from the official report he provided for the police on November 10, 1975:

"Deanna and I walked out of the dorm and down past the library. As we were walking by I noticed a guy with a sling standing near the bicycle rack in front of the library. My attention was drawn to him because he had his left arm in a dark blue sling and I'd never seen one that color."

Barnard then goes on to describe him, how tall he was, his approximate weight, and what he was wearing. He told police that later that night, after attending a portion of Deanna's anthropology class, he again saw Bundy:

"Later that evening, Deanna had an anthropology class in Barge Hall. I went to the first part of the class but got bored and left at the break which was around 8:00 p.m. The class was from 7:00 to 9:30. I walked over to the Arctic Circle [an area on campus] and as I was walking back to Barge Hall to get Deanna, I saw the same guy with the sling out in front of Barge Hall. He wasn't talking to anyone, but I got the impression he may have been smoking with his right hand."

During our phone conversation, Barnard also mentioned that he believed Bundy had books on the ground next to him.

To get an idea of where these locations are in relation to each other, the library is on Walnut Street, and Barge Hall is on Eighth Avenue. This means that Bundy had to walk about one-half block down Walnut, turn right on Eighth and continue walking two blocks before he reached Barge Hall, where he'd be seen again by Barnard. This was approximately 9:30 p.m. This was the last time Kent Barnard would see the man with the sling. That is, it was the last time he would see him and realize it.

A little over 30 minutes later, Susan Rancourt would encounter Bundy as she left Munson Hall, which sits on the corner of Walnut Street and Eighth Avenue. Again, from my book:

"At 10:15, as Barbara Blair was crossing Walnut Street at Eighth Avenue (the location of Munson Hall and close to the library, which is also on Walnut), she saw a man 'in a green ski parka, who acted as though he were in a daze,' as well as a young white female 'wearing a yellow low coat going north on the Walnut Mall.'"

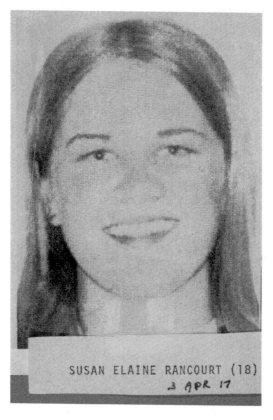

SUSAN ELAINE RANCOURT (18)
3 APR 17

Susan Rancourt was a happy and hardworking girl on the night she disappeared in a darkened and somewhat remote area of Central Washington State College (courtesy King County Archives).

That female was Susan Rancourt, and it may be that as Bundy walked the two blocks back to Walnut Street, he hovered at the intersection, for by doing this he'd have a good view not only of the library and all the foot traffic going up and down Walnut, but what was happening on Eighth Avenue as well. By ruse, he convinced Susan to follow him, down Walnut, past the library, over the bridge running next to the library, and then they would angle off to the left past the side of Black Hall while they kept walking towards the desolate area where his VW was parked next to the railroad trestle.

Perhaps the most chilling sight Kent Barnard caught that night (though he didn't know it at the time, of course) was during his drive back to Seattle:

"I drove back to Seattle later that night by way of I-90. About 10 miles east of Issaquah, I saw a set of small round taillights about 200 yards up a logging road on the north side of I-90."

This would have been Bundy's Volkswagen, containing (no doubt) the unconscious Susan Rancourt, whom Bundy would kill there.

Kent Barnard has thought a lot about that day over the years. He's thought about Bundy and his ruse of using the sling. His mind has also drifted back to the small glowing taillights he'd spotted on that deserted logging road, and he's thought about Susan Rancourt. And, I suspect, for the remainder of his life, his mind will occasionally take that journey back to April 17, 1974, and what he saw at Central Washington State College.

An interesting aspect of writing true crime book is the people who contact you *after* your book is published. More often than not, they will be friends of the murdered, and no matter who it is or what they want to tell me, I always welcome the contact. Indeed, I come away from it a richer person, as I feel as though I know their slain friend or family member as well. In fact, there isn't a day that goes by that I don't think about the victims of Ted Bundy and the case in general. It's just the way it is when you write such a book. But I did have one contact that would have a special meaning for me. Her name was Lorraine Fargo, and she not only was a friend of Kathy Parks but also was the last person to talk to that young woman before she was beguiled by Ted Bundy and taken away forever.

On the evening of Monday, May 6, 1974, Ted Bundy was hunting for a young woman at Oregon State University in Corvallis. The trip to Oregon was an attempt, he would later tell investigators, to throw off the police investigating the killings in Washington. His day would be a long and tiring one: A 250-mile road trip just to reach the campus, a hunt that could take any number of hours, and then the long haul back. Not to mention the probable sexual attack on his upcoming victim once he'd captured her, and the repeated sexual assaults prior to her murder once he'd reached his destination. All of this would take time, and Ted Bundy was willing to give it his all. Murder was in his blood, and it was all he now thought about.

Kathy Parks had started her day on a down note: Her father had had a heart attack, but the good news was that he was recovering. As such, she didn't leave school and travel back home to California. Her sister, who was married and living in Nevada, would keep her apprised of his improvement, and so Kathy felt good about staying at OSU.

Her dad wasn't the only thing on her mind. She was not doing as well lately with her classes, and, by her own admission, she'd been drinking too much. She was also having problems with her boyfriend, Christy McPhee, a scuba diving instructor from Berwick, Louisiana. He wanted to settle down, but she didn't. Still, he was set to visit her in Oregon and she was looking forward to seeing him.

Kathy Parks, vulnerable and still trying to figure out her life, met Bundy late one night in the cafeteria of Oregon State University and simply vanished (courtesy King County Archives).

There is a definite sadness in some of her surviving photographs, though certainly not the one I've chosen for this book, and from the record, her moodiness might have been a constant companion in her life. She also had the habit of walking alone on the darkened campus at night, visiting the Memorial Union Commons cafeteria usually between 9:00 and 11:00 p.m. She would invite others to join her on these nocturnal strolls but, apparently, didn't have a lot of takers. On the night of May 6, she would again head out into the night.

Leaving Sackett Hall, she journeyed down the sidewalk, and just before she reached Memorial Union Commons, she ran into her friend, Lorraine Fargo. What follows is from my previous Ted Bundy book. There are two places where I surmise something might have happened, and, for this publication only, those portions are italicized:

"At a few minutes past 11, Lorraine Fargo, another friend, saw Kathy walking alone and would tell police: 'She appeared to be dazed and in a dream.' It was a chance meeting, as Lorraine was on her way back to Sackett Hall after an evening of studying at the library. It was warm and clear that night, and as the two of them stood there, Lorraine listened as Kathy expressed her desire to 'be on her own [and that] she did not want any obligations, and did not want to continue [her] relationship on a permanent basis.' Lorraine, who had recently ended a relationship and could see how depressed she was, asked Kathy to break off the walk and come back to her place so they could talk about it. But Kathy, she said, 'just felt like being alone, taking a walk, and trying to straighten things out in her own mind.' She also admitted to having skipped her classes that week, and that she had been drinking too much.

"It is unknown exactly when her killer first spotted her. Perhaps it was while she was eating in the cafeteria, and he sat down beside her and began to talk? Or he may have seen her stop and speak with Lorraine. *Maybe he'd been following Lorraine and noticed the distraught coed with the pretty, waist-length hair and decided he wanted her instead.* Perhaps he could see the vulnerability in her countenance. No one knows for sure."

I also surmise in my previous book that the letter she sent to her boyfriend may have been mailed during that walk. Again, from my book: *"Because the letter bears a May 7 postmark, it may have been mailed that evening, possibly placed in a mail box just a short time before her disappearance."*

Now, what is above in italics are assumptions I made based on things I knew about Bundy, and what I believed may have happened. Of course, there was no way to know this for a certainty, so I included it in my book as a possibility only. In my mind, it was a very good possibility, of course, but that was all.

And then, about a year after my book was published, Lorraine Fargo contacted me. I must admit that after hearing from her I was both surprised and extremely pleased, and I responded immediately. And from the moment we began exchanging emails, it was like we were old friends. It also became clear Lorraine carried damage from the events of 1974, and she admitted that Ted Bundy had always been a touchy subject for her. I told her that I understood perfectly, and that most of the friends of the murdered feel the same way. All in all, however, she knew that reading my book and communicating with me would be cathartic, and that it was now the proper time to let that occur. Not only did she share much information with me, but she actually got up the nerve to answer questions on a Ted Bundy blog that I chair.

What follows are words from Lorraine Fargo concerning the night that Kathy Parks disappeared:

"I avoided reading most of the media hype regarding Ted Bundy during the time he was first arrested. As a kid, I loved things like 'The Alfred Hitchcock Hour' and 'The Legend of Hill House,' but once something bizarre and terrifying becomes a part of your reality, it's hard to find similar topics 'entertaining.' Part of me really wanted to read about Bundy, because I had so many unanswered questions, but the other, more protective part, didn't dare. In 1986 I was working as a fish processor aboard the MV Galaxy in Dutch Harbor, Alaska. One Friday night one of the movies about Bundy was being shown in the galley. I think it was 'The Stranger Beside Me' but can't be sure. I watched about 20 minutes of it and became nauseated, and returned to my room.

"Anyway, it was not until I read the excerpt from Kevin's book that I made the 'library' connection. I couldn't help but notice, in his writing, that in many of Bundy's 1st abductions and attempted abductions, he and his victims were in or near a university library. Well... I had been studying at the library the night that Kathy was abducted, and I did have a slightly strange experience while I was there.

"There was this guy who seemed to be EVERYWHERE I was. I had a lot to do to complete my report, due the following day, and I was in 'serious study mode.' When I went to the card catalog, there was a guy standing next to me looking through a different drawer. When I went to find the books on the shelves, he was again, right next to me, searching the shelves. He said something to the effect of 'I can never find what I'm looking for here...' I pretty much ignored him, having found what I needed, and went to a table to begin working. A few minutes later he came and sat down at the same table, opposite side, a few chairs over. He asked if I had an extra pen, which I gave him. I proceeded to work, and he started to speak again. I said 'Excuse me, but I have a ton of work to do,' and I gathered up my stuff and went to another table. [*I believe this indeed could have been Ted Bundy. We can't say absolutely, but given his penchant*

for hunting university libraries, it is more than possible.]
"I was annoyed because I had a lot to do, but didn't think much more than that. It was getting late and they had announced that the library was closing soon. As I prepared to leave, I noticed the same guy, a short distance away. I remember being creeped out enough to take the stairs (in a group of students) rather than the elevator, and making sure I exited the library's front door with a number of other students. I stayed very close to a group headed in the same direction that was slightly ahead of me. They crossed the street right about the time I spotted Kathy. I was very close to the dorm at that point, and there were still several people walking in the vicinity, so I pretty much forgot about 'the guy' and proceeded on to Sackett Hall after talking with Kathy.

"I also didn't realize, until reading Kevin's book, that the letter Christy received from Kathy, dated May 7th, 1974, was ever questioned. Kathy, in fact, had that letter in her hand as we spoke, and I watched her mail it in the small mailbox in front of the Commons just after we parted. The place we met and talked was just across the street from the Commons.... her destination after we spoke was no more than 50 feet away."

Lorraine Fargo also related that when their conversation ended, she continued walking toward Sackett Hall and Kathy ventured on across a little campus street to the Memorial Union Commons, placed the letter in the mailbox, and continued up the steps and into the cafeteria. Soon after this, Bundy (as if on cue) came into the cafeteria and introduced himself, and like always, by ruse, convinced Kathy Parks to follow him to her death. After he had her out of town, he took control of her, no doubt bound her, and the two made the long drive back to Seattle, probably not arriving until at least 4:00 a.m. Because of the lateness of the hour, Bundy would almost certainly have killed her shortly after their arrival.

Steve Costa, who also contacted me after reading my book, and who would later go into law enforcement, remembers Kathy when she was a student at Diablo Valley College in their home state of California:

"Kathy and I were classmates at Diablo Valley College in Pleasant Hill, California, in 1972/1973. Kathy was majoring in Liberal Arts at the time. I remember the first time I saw her in Humanities class, I looked at her and our eyes met. I looked into those deep blue eyes and I just melted, for I thought she was incredibly beautiful. She was the textbook visage of the All-American Girl, clean cut and well dressed with waist length, ash blonde hair and deep blue eyes. She looked like the type of girl that you would have been proud to take home and meet your parents. Kathy's personality, however, was far more complex than her appearance. She exhibited a demure, reserved demeanor, almost sullen on many occasions. It looked like she was brooding over something or that something was troubling her. She rarely smiled and was a hard person to try and talk to. She rarely spoke out in class. I was very much attracted to her looks, but her withdrawn personality kept me at bay...She later transferred up to Oregon State University in Corvallis, Oregon, to pursue her studies in Liberal Arts and World Religions."

When you visit today, Oregon State University looks as inviting as it did when Lorraine Fargo and Kathy Parks had that late-night conversation in the spring of 1974. Sackett Hall is virtually the same, and the Union Commons stands as it did at that time, although the inside may have been refurbished a bit. The mailbox that once stood on the sidewalk near the steps of the commons has been removed, but other than that, all parties involved would recognize the locations today.

Bundy's return to his regular hunting grounds in Washington meant that more women were going to die. Brenda Carol Ball, 22, would, like all of Bundy's victims, slip away from the Earth both quickly and unexpectedly. Her final night of life was spent at the Flame Tavern, located at 12803 Ambaum Blvd. SW in Burien, just south of Seattle. Bundy would later confirm he killed her (in *The Bundy Murders* I included the odd conversation Bundy had with Liz Kendall about Ball's murder). Today, the Flame is long gone, but the building survives as a Mexican restaurant.

Georgann Hawkins was pretty, friendly, and willing to help the injured man she encountered in the alleyway running behind her sorority house (courtesy King County Archives).

The abduction and murder of Georgann Hawkins occurred in the early morning hours of June 11, 1974. A pretty girl with a great personality (literally, everybody liked her), Georg (pronounced George) was ending her freshman year at the University of Washington with a 3.5 GPA. That said, she was having some concern about a Spanish test scheduled for the next day, and had spent much of the previous evening studying. But she did take a break about 9:30 p.m. to visit a frat party several blocks away. And after a couple of hours, and a like number of beers, she and a friend made the short walk back to their UW sorority house on what's known as Greek Row, using the alley in the rear of the buildings to walk home.

And then, perhaps on a whim, she decided to visit her boyfriend in his fraternity house on the corner, leaving her friend to walk by herself a short distance before she could enter their home. Even so, Georgann waited until her friend had safely passed through the door before she entered the frat house to see her boyfriend.

In retrospect, it's all a matter of chance, really. Had Bundy not been operating in this area on what the killer would later tell detectives was "a warm Seattle May night," we would never have heard the name Georgann Hawkins. She no doubt would be alive today, perhaps with children and grandchildren. But evil was coming toward her and there just wasn't any way for her to know it.

As Georgann later left the building through the rear door leading into the alleyway (the same door she'd entered earlier), she intended to walk quickly to the sorority house so she could once again immerse herself in the Spanish language. Duane Covey heard the door close from his room on the second floor of the fraternity house, and jumped up to see who was leaving. Spotting Georgann, he called out and the two stood and talked awhile. As they did, he later reported that they heard laughter coming from somewhere down the alley in the direction of Georgann's sorority house. Georgann turned to look down the alley a couple of times but didn't see anyone. That laughter came from Ted Bundy.

After Georgann and Duane said goodbye in Spanish, she headed down the alley and passed into the darkness. Duane naturally walked away from his window. Within minutes, however, Georgann would emerge from the darkness of the alleyway with someone who was a stranger to her. She was carrying a briefcase while the dark-haired man hobbled on crutches. As they reached the end of the alley, they turned right, walked the short distance to Seventeenth Street NE, and immediately turned left and walked the short distance to a dimly-lighted parking lot where his VW was parked. It was now a little before 1:00 a.m.

Within moments of being at the car, as Georgann was reaching inside the passenger side door (no doubt to lay the briefcase on the back seat), Ted Bundy picked up the crowbar he'd placed behind the left rear tire, and quickly slammed it into her head. Indeed, he hit her with such force that Georgann came out of one shoe and both earrings flew onto the gravel parking lot. These pieces of evidence would be gathered up by Bundy the next day even as a hornets' nest of cops were swarming the area, gathering evidence only a block away. Riding his bicycle, Bundy passed through the area like a ghost, and no one paid any attention to him.

If you visit these sites today, they look as warm and inviting as they did on that warm summer evening in June of 1974. Greek Row looks much the same, as does the alleyway running behind it. The parking lot is still there, but it's paved now and has a basketball stand with hoop and net permanently affixed. There's also a newer building right next to it (I was told it was built about ten years ago), and some additions that would not have been there when Bundy led Georgann to his VW.

It is of interest to note too, that while it was a deserted parking lot where Bundy could attack her with relative ease, there were, directly across from the narrow alley, a row of buildings filled with windows from which anyone could have been looking out. The lack of light obviously helped Bundy, and, despite the possibility of prying eyes, he got away with it.

He would place the body of Georgann Hawkins at what would become known as the Issaquah dump site. Joining her in the near future at this same location would be his Lake Sammamish victims, Janice Ott and Denise Naslund.

The double daylight abduction at Lake Sammamish on July 14, 1974, was a jaw-dropping act from a killer desiring to make a statement about who he was and the power he could wield. From Bundy's smug perspective, it was smooth sailing all the way, and there wasn't, in his mind, any reason not to attempt it. And once again, he would be successful in carrying out his plans and would not be apprehended either in the act or anytime in the near future. However, he would leave his "imprint" while there in the form of his description, his make of car, and, unbelievably, his real name. His confidence level being what it was, it's no wonder he was so careless while there. It was clear his contempt for the authorities was rising, and Lake Sammamish would confirm in the killer's mind that all of his actions were correct. They weren't, of course, but his mindset on that day was one of invincibility.

July 14 that year was hot and sunny, and the crowd at Lake Sammamish State Park would swell to some 40,000 people. There were various company picnics, and even the cops were having an organized event. With such a sea of humanity all around, it would not be (in the minds of most people) the place one would stage a kidnapping--much less two abductions on the same day.

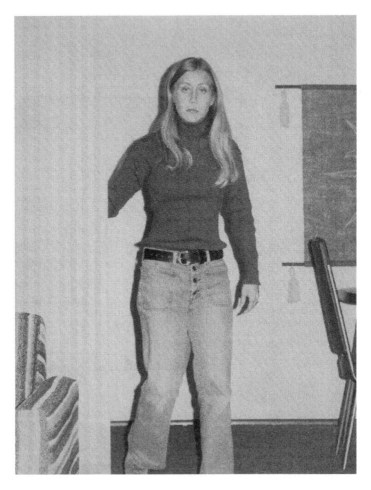

Janice Ott, a resident of Issaquah, rode her bicycle to Lake Sammamish on the Morning of July 14, 1974, and soon fell victim to Bundy's lies (courtesy King County Archives)

Denise Naslund, who encountered Bundy late in the
afternoon at Lake Sammamish, became his second and last
victim of the day (courtesy King County Archives)

In any event, Bundy would convince Janice Ott, who
was twenty-three, to leave with him after he conned her by
way of a ruse. And later, after he was tired from dealing

45

with that captured prey all day, he returned to the park and tricked eighteen-year-old Denise Naslund to go with him to her death. Having taken control of her, he took Denise to where Janice was still being kept, bound up but alive and experiencing a great deal of terror and mental anguish.

Indeed, one can easily imagine the fear for both women as they understood it was unlikely they would survive the ordeal. And after repeated sexual attacks (first with Ott and then Naslund), Bundy killed one in front of the other, which of course would cause an unthinkable wave of horror to engulf the one who witnessed it. We do not know how long the interval of time, but after awhile, Bundy killed his second Lake Sam victim and disposed of their remains.

A footnote to these particular killings: There were times when Bundy was murdering a young woman when he would not want her to be conscious. He wanted her alive, but not looking at him or conversing with him. His unconscious victims, those he'd bashed in the head with a tire iron one, two or three times, were for Bundy little more than playthings. His normal method of killing his victims was having intercourse from behind, either anal or vaginal, while they were still breathing, and he would slowly choke them to death with either an electrical cord (his preferred tool for strangulation), or perhaps a piece of rope. During these times the women would die without fear as they were already unconscious. But there were times, as with the Lake Sammamish murders, where he wanted his victims to experience the most extreme terror possible. Like a madman, Ted Bundy would drink in such a moment and make it his own. It was fuel to him.

And yet, after the publication of *The Bundy Murders*, some people actually contacted me to explain how wrong I was about that, that Ted Bundy had stated he didn't want people "to suffer," and because of this, it couldn't be true. Such thinking, of course, is contrary to the record and all the known facts and what Bundy himself would later say about the murders.

In any event, visitors to Lake Sammamish State Park today will find it looking very much like it did on the day Ted Bundy would forever link himself with this beautiful resort area. As you enter the park, and just before it opens up to the parking lot, if you look to your left, you'll see a restroom still standing and still in use from that time. A nearly identical restroom at the far end of the park (the one Bundy was stalking when he encountered Denise Naslund) has been torn down.

Standing practically in the middle of the park sits a curved, long rectangular building that housed the concession stand and additional bathrooms. On the side of this structure, recessed in concrete, is the name "Lake Sammamish," so that the onlookers never forget where they are. In light of what happened here over 40 years ago, it is impossible for anyone familiar with the Bundy case to forget this place. As long as these murders Bundy committed are studied, Lake Sammamish will be a big part of it, such was the shock that not just one but two young women were led away to their deaths from this very pleasant and family-friendly state park.

When my wife and I visited the site in July 2015, I had just one thing on my mind: envisioning what it must have been like on that hot July day in 1974. Although it was both sunny and beautiful while we were there (just like the day Denise Naslund and Janice Ott were taken), there was hardly a soul in sight. But my mind was racing back through the years for the immense crowd that was at the lake that day. Standing at the approximate spot Janice Ott was sitting when she encountered Ted, I imagined the two of them talking, and I kept thinking about how innocent it all must have seemed to Janice, and how normal Ted must have appeared to her. And then the image slowly faded away, and I was back in 2015.

Farther down in the park was where Denise Naslund had been with her boyfriend and friends, and it's as if this section forever belongs to her. Standing there, taking it all in, it's easy to "see" how it all went down that day, and it's still astonishing to me that Ted Bundy would have exposed himself to so many witnesses while hunting women to kill.

Before we leave the murders of Washington behind, I would be remiss if I didn't touch upon the relationship Ted Bundy had with the late writer Ann Rule. At the time they worked together as telephone crisis counselors in Seattle, she had not yet become a prolific and well-known writer of true crime.

I never met Ann Rule, but I would have liked to, if only to discuss the Bundy case with her. Indeed, if you know the Bundy murders even slightly, chances are you're aware of the connection between them, and that connection gave birth to her best-selling book, *The Stranger Beside Me*, about her relationship with the killer.

Throughout the years that Bundy was incarcerated (beginning in Utah), they exchanged letters, phone calls, and she even attended his trials in Florida. Some of Bundy's letters to Rule made their way into the official record, and I will use two of them at the end of the book in a short chapter titled "Bundy: A Man of Letters."

During my visit with my wife to Washington in July 2015, I didn't understand how ill Ann Rule really was at the time. I'd heard she had been in the hospital, but for a person of 83 years, that isn't all that unusual. And then, somewhat oddly, I found myself thinking about her on several occasions that month as I photographed and walked the locations of Bundy's murder trail throughout the state. Although I wondered why it was happening, each time it occurred I let it go. And then, within a week after returning from the Pacific Northwest, we, along with the rest of the world, heard the news of her passing.

CHAPTER TWO
An Expanding Evil: 1974 - 1975

A waitress who'd worked at Denny's on Sixth Avenue in Tacoma, Washington, saw Ted Bundy quite often before he became infamous, as he was a regular at the restaurant. She recently told me that he looked like a lawyer, spoke well, and was always polite. In other words, there was nothing about his demeanor that gave her pause, or caused her to be even the slightest bit suspicious that he was anything other than what he revealed himself to be every time he walked through the door. Needless to say, after the world was introduced to the real Ted Bundy, she couldn't bring herself to believe it, and she wouldn't be alone. Most greeted this unveiling with a sense of shock and disbelief; almost like a bad dream from which they could not awake. Ted Bundy couldn't be responsible for the attacking, abducting and murdering of women, they thought. Oh no. Not this Ted.

When Bundy left Washington, he managed to escape the investigators on his trail unscathed. Despite the round-the-clock efforts by King County Police Detective Bob Keppel and his team, the very bold killer remained a mystery to them. Not one piece of evidence had been obtained that could lead them to their man, and the investigators understood that the killer might, at any time, simply leave the state for another killing ground--and that's exactly what happened.

From Bundy's perspective, it was without question time

to go. He understood they were looking for someone named "Ted" who drove a Volkswagen. This may not have troubled him a great deal, but the connection might be made. He'd already made one attempt to throw investigators off his trail, as he would later tell a writer, by driving to Oregon to snatch and kill Kathy Parks. And besides, he reasoned, Utah offered a fresh killing ground and also the perfect cover, as he'd be attending the University of Utah School of Law.

Because Bundy loved murder above all things, when he spotted the pretty young woman with the green backpack standing on the freeway entrance ramp on the outskirts of Boise, Idaho, he pulled his VW into the emergency lane and within a second, the doomed young woman was inside his cramped car, chatting away with the smiling and handsome man who would soon kill her.

They were travelling down Interstate 84 and, according to Bundy, they rode together for the next three or four hours. At the time, I-84 was broken up into modern sections of new highway and the older road still undergoing construction. And at some point, after it was dark, Bundy exited I-84 and followed a road that led to the nearby river, a river he said he'd been eyeing for a while.

Soon, Bundy would send the tire iron crashing into the back of his victim's head, and, once parked, he'd drag her unconscious body to a spot he deemed good enough to undress her and sexually assault her. True to his MO, he would strangle the young hitchhiker (who remains unknown) while having intercourse, either vaginal or anal, from behind. And, because he loved necrophilia, the killer would stay with her for a while, admiring his "work" while he enjoyed the changes he saw occurring in her body. After additional acts of copulation, Bundy slid her body into the river and returned to his car. He still had a long drive ahead of him, and Bundy wouldn't arrive at his new home at 565 First Ave.

in Salt Lake City until the wee hours of the morning.

Bundy revealed the facts of this abduction during his end-of-life confessions while imprisoned in Florida. That was the first time he would come clean with the detectives from the respective states who were trying to close cases of missing and murdered women that had been connected to Bundy. And it's evident from all the statements he made--to Utah Detective Dennis Couch, Lead Investigator Russ Reneau of Idaho, Lead Detective Bob Keppel from Washington, and Lead Investigator Mike Fisher from Colorado--that he was willing to talk freely about these murders. As such, they are the most trusted of all the confessions, and in my mind, supersede all previous "confessions" because he knew he'd be required to release valid, important and, ultimately, provable information. And in this respect, Bundy kept his promise.

With this in mind, when I was doing research about Bundy's travels through Idaho during his move to Utah on September 2, 1974 (I was actually the first Bundy biographer to locate and publish his exact date of departure from Seattle), I had the transcript of Bundy's hour-long confession to investigators Russ Reneau and Randy Everitt. In the transcript of that session, conducted on January 22, 1989 (two days before his execution), I quickly discovered the complete story of the murder of the Idaho hitchhiker. Until my book was published, very little was known about this murder, and most writers reference the murder only. However, not only did I have the transcript–Bundy's last word on the murders prior to his execution–but I was faced with choosing between this (what I believed to be the actual account) and a story Bundy told a psychiatrist many months earlier that was *a radically different story about the murder!*

Why would Bundy give two different scenarios concerning this murder? Who knows? But reading the transcript of the confession in which he admits not just to the murder of the hitchhiker, but also offers a detailed explanation of the murder of twelve-year-old Lynette Culver--with a promise to help investigators should further answers be needed--I believed (and still do believe) that this was the truth being told for the first time with the publication of *The Bundy Murders*. It's baffling to me why Bundy would have given such an elaborate untruth to those who were trying desperately to help him, but in my opinion this is exactly what happened. Now, someone might be inclined to ask: "Well, could he have killed a second hitchhiker in Idaho?" And in my mind, the answer to that would be no.

When Bundy arrived in Salt Lake City, he was in somewhat familiar territory, something that he enjoyed. He'd been in the city and other locations in Utah because of his ongoing relationship with his girlfriend, Liz Kendall, a native of the state. In Utah he could feel a bit like he was home, and he'd find the time to work in such normal things as seeing Liz's folks as he fulfilled his murderous desires. In fact, he went hunting in late October 1974 with Liz's father only hours after abducting a young woman named Melissa Smith, the daughter of Midvale Chief of Police Louis Smith. While Bundy was hunting non-human game, he kept Melissa safely ensconced in his apartment at 565 First Ave., still alive but bound and probably in a coma. Bundy would eventually kill the young woman, as he did with all his victims, and dump her body near a subdivision where he knew she'd be found. (Yes, there were times when Bundy wanted his victims located, and other times when he wanted them hidden away forever.)

It is important to understand the mindset of Ted Bundy in his new home: Being in Utah was about enjoying a brand new killing ground. It was a fresh opportunity to hunt young women without law enforcement constantly trying to get in the way, as they were now doing back in Seattle and throughout the state of Washington. Indeed, as Bundy drove away from Seattle on that September day in 1974, he was leaving the hottest manhunt the Pacific Northwest had ever experienced, either before or since.

His friends (and this includes his girlfriend Liz Kendall) in Washington believed his departure from that state was all about attending the University of Utah School of Law, as Bundy had withdrawn from, in his mind, the less esteemed School of Law at the University of Puget Sound. But studying the law, as anything more than a cover for his diabolical activities, no longer mattered. Bundy wasn't going to be a lawyer, and any political aspirations he'd previously entertained were a mirage that had totally and forever vanished.

He was a full-time killer now and nothing more. He lived and breathed murder, and if Washington had taught his twisted mind anything it was that he could take his prey at will and there was nothing the authorities could do about it. But Utah would be Bundy's Waterloo; his unmasking would begin in the Beehive State, and, when this happened, things would change dramatically in his life.

Concerning his behavior in Utah, I wrote this in *The Bundy Murders*:

"So it is quite clear that rather than attending law classes, Ted Bundy was driving hundreds of miles around the metropolitan area seeking victims and familiarizing himself with the many connecting smaller towns and suburbs, as well as the more rural environs of his new home. Although he had scanned some of this with a predatory eye with Liz prior to moving here, nothing compared to spending entire days and evenings alone, diligently roaming about in his attempt to memorize the land in much the same way he came to both fully know and use to such great effect those deserted, brush-covered places so seemingly void of habitability back in Washington State."

Like a kid in a candy store, Bundy was having the time of his life.

In Utah (just as he had in Washington), Bundy would seek out high-caliber friends, and he would rub shoulders with those who were on track to some very good places in life. He would fit in well, as he always had, and no one would suspect he was anything other than a transplanted law student from Washington.

One aspect of Bundy's activities in Utah was his association with members of the Mormon Church, both men and women. Those who knew Bundy in this "world" found him to be seemingly normal and kind, someone, in their mind, who would make a perfect member of their church. And their reaction to Bundy was no different than any other group of folks who interacted with him. Ted Bundy knew how to treat people and mix with them in ways that would cause them to not just accept him but genuinely like him and want his friendship. In an article published in the *Deseret News* on January 24, 1989 (the day Bundy was executed), staff writer Ellen Fagg interviewed Mel Thayne of the Church of Jesus Christ of Latter-day Saints (LDS). The following quotes are taken directly from that article:

"'All my memories of him are quite positive,' said Mel Thayne, then bishop of an LDS student branch Bundy actively attended. 'The girls were quite taken with him, and the fellows liked him, too. He just impressed all of us. ... He commented he would like to see what a Mormon family in our own setting was like. He had commented on what lovely girls we had.'"

At the time Bundy was getting to know the family, the Thaynes had four teenage daughters.

In retrospect, Thayne's wife, Emma Lou, said: "It kind

of gives you the shivers when you think of what might have been."

Of course, Bundy had not been faithful to Liz Kendall in Washington, and Utah would be no different. And when contemplating Ted Bundy, we must always remember he was a user of people, especially women. It didn't matter if they were victims, girlfriends, or friends, he would take advantage of them all. With the victims he would assault them sexually, murder them, and sexually abuse them after death. With other women, he would use them sexually and he always managed to become a magnet for their money. It was always the same old story with Ted. But of course, he did everything he could to keep this hidden from the people who were being used.

There is an interesting photograph of Bundy and a young blonde woman named Carol Hall, doing the dishes together at a party in Salt Lake City. It's a photo that's been seen by millions of people, and it was taken merely by chance, at a party that should have been remembered only by the attendees. But one-half of that picture was about to be exposed to the world, and forever after it would no longer be any ordinary photograph.

During the research for this book, I was able to locate the woman in that photograph, Carol Hall Bartholomew, and she very kindly shared her story with me concerning that photo and her personal knowledge of Ted Bundy. What follows is the story in Carol's own words, and because of the length of the email I have used italics:

The year was 1974. I was an elementary school teacher who had temporarily left my teaching career to return to the University of Utah to earn a Master of Education Degree. I began attending church in a "student branch" (a congregation of the Church of Jesus

Christ of Latter-day Saints, comprised of unmarried college students). It was there that I met four young men who shared an apartment not far from my home: Wynn Bartholomew, John Homer, Larry Anderson, and Barry Kraus. Wynn was attending law school at the University of Utah. The apartment where these four men lived was quite large, and became the "social center" or "gathering place" for many of the members of our branch: We went there often for parties.

John Homer and Larry Anderson were "stake missionaries" at the time. One day Wynn told John and Larry about a student at the Law School who was possibly a potential convert and who might be interested in having religious discussions with them; his name was Ted Bundy. John and Larry began giving religious lessons to Ted at their apartment. They invited Ted to come to church and meet the rest of the congregation; Ted was always invited to the apartment for social gatherings as well.

Eventually Ted committed to being baptized. Many members of the student branch attended the baptism to show their support. Our branch president, Michael Preece, interviewed Ted prior to baptism ... John Homer performed the baptism and his missionary companion, Larry Anderson, pronounced the confirmation. Little did anyone know what dark secrets Ted was hiding!

And then, Carol begins to recount an aspect of the student branch membership that would have been noticed by Bundy and would have acted as a drawing card for the killer:

The ratio of women to men in our student branch was about 4 to 1, so new men coming to our branch were always of interest, and Ted was no exception. He was polite, courteous, intelligent, and attractive. Many of the young women wanted to date Ted; he became quite popular in our group. Ted attended some of our social gatherings, and afterwards, Wynn remembered that to him, Ted seemed quiet and mysterious; at social gatherings he would sit in the background and just watch people silently.

Carol also speaks of the time in early 1975, during the winter months, when Bundy missed some of his activities with the church. At that time, unbeknown to them, he was out committing murders next door in Colorado ...

John Homer and Larry Anderson asked Wynn about Ted; they said that he had missed an appointment with them to have another religious discussion, and they wondered if Wynn had seen Ted at the Law School. During Winter Quarter it was very unusual for a student to go out of town, due to winter weather conditions. Wynn remembers that it was odd that Ted was absent from school at the time. When Ted did return to Law School, Wynn remembers noticing that Ted looked rather weather-worn and had four evenly-spaced scratch marks on the side of his face, and asked him about it. Ted blew it off by saying that he had been scratched by a tree branch ...

In March of 1975, I organized a birthday party for one of our branch members, Sam Green; the party was held at Wynn's apartment. I was busy washing dishes when Ted walked over and stood beside me. "You look like you could use some help" he offered. I was flattered that he would notice me, and hoped that perhaps he would ask me out on a date. My camera was sitting nearby, and I handed it to Wynn and asked, "Wynn, take my picture with Ted!" Ted pointed a rinsing gun at me as we posed together. It was one of the few pictures taken of Ted outside a courtroom or jail.

58

Carol believes that the picture may actually have saved her life: If anything had happened to her, she reasons, Bundy might just have been viewed as a suspect in the disappearance, as the picture was a clear link between the two of them. That same month, Carol and Wynn began dating, and that dating led to a marriage that produced a family of six sons, five daughters in law, and many grandchildren. Wynn, who was a loving husband, father, and grandfather, and who had a career practicing law, passed away in April 2013.

It is interesting to note that while Bundy immersed himself in the church and easily mingled with members at social functions, he still often managed to be somewhat aloof. Wynn's observation that Ted was "quiet and mysterious" and that he would sit silently and watch people, speaks a great deal about him in hindsight: He was the always observing predator. Nevertheless, Ted was popular wherever he went, and this included social functions, be they with a church group or in the midst of a raucous crowd in a tavern. Ted fit in, plain and simple.

He was also a very good actor.

In my book *The Bundy Murders*, I describe at length the principal characteristics of the psychopath, and what such individuals must do to function in life. Bundy, the quintessential homicidal psychopath, adopted early in life a mask–an outer self--to conceal his inner inadequacies, and he was very successful at doing so. As such, when he became a killer, he understood the supreme importance of concealing not just his activities from the authorities and the public at large, but also to have the mask in place in such a way that even his closest friends would never suspect him. And he would continue to be very good at this deception until his meltdown in Florida.

John Homer has interesting remembrances of Ted Bundy as well. He recalls Bundy as being well-liked. While sometimes Bundy would keep to himself, Homer says, Ted was never rude or awkward socially. On the contrary, Bundy would always join in conversations, and Homer felt that Ted was a very smart guy as he always seemed to have an answer for any of the questions being tossed about the room. As can be expected, they were shocked when Bundy was arrested for the abduction of Carol DaRonch in October of 1975.

Even so, the knowledge of what he was would not come easy to any of them, no matter what the authorities thought, as his demeanor didn't fit the pattern of an abductor and killer of women. Still, believing in their friend's innocence, they did not give up on Bundy, and John would visit him at the Salt Lake County Jail, would attend four days of his five-day trial, and would visit him again at the Utah State Prison after his conviction.

The trial was rather unusual, inasmuch as it was a bench trial. This meant that there would be no jury of a dozen Utahans, who would debate the evidence, and might not come up with a decision to convict. As Homer remembered it, "Bundy elected to waive his right to a trial by jury, because of the emotional nature of the crime of which he was accused. He felt he could do better with the judge." Bundy's fate, therefore, rested in the hands of Judge Stewart M. Hanson, and he alone would decide, based on the evidence, what would happen to the accused law student. Without question, Judge Hanson was a fair man and well-respected throughout his community. It was somewhat risky for Bundy, who apparently thought it an acceptable risk.

During the trial, which began on Monday, February 23, 1976, Homer and Bundy were able to exchange words occasionally. And on Thursday--the trial would end the next day--Homer, who had to leave town and wouldn't be in court the next day, joked to Bundy, "Been nice knowing you, Ted.

Have a nice rest of your life" and both men laughed.

But when John Homer learned that Bundy had been convicted, he was shocked. Not only did he believe Ted was innocent, but he (as did others) believed that the defense provided enough evidence to place Bundy in that all-important category of reasonable doubt. But Judge Hanson, who, after absorbing all of the evidence during that week and contemplating and reviewing all the evidence yet again in his mind over the weekend, came to the definite conclusion that Theodore Bundy was in fact guilty of the abduction of Carol DaRonch. And his sentence, pronounced in the coming days, meant he would spend one to fifteen years at the Utah State Prison.

When John Homer visited Bundy prior to the conviction, he was being housed at the Salt Lake County Jail. He said his first meeting with Ted was a somber one. Bundy, understanding his dire situation, knew his options were limited. When Homer asked what he planned to do, Bundy responded "I don't know. I have no money." This led John, along with Wynn Bartholomew and other housemates, to try and raise money for Bundy. Of course, they were young college kids with limited assets. Still, they managed to collect several hundred dollars for Bundy. In today's money, that's a couple thousand dollars.

When Homer met with Bundy at the Utah State Prison, he remembers Ted saying something that was odd, and totally out of character to what kind of person he believed him to be. Bundy, obviously in a rotten mood, quipped "I could get out of this prison if I wanted to," and then spoke some "disparaging remarks about the guards, and told me about some corridors that were not guarded." Such talk, John Homer believed, was not like the Ted he'd come to know and call a friend, and it made an impression on him.

Belief in the goodness of Ted, however, would change

drastically in the coming weeks of 1976 for all involved. According to Homer, one of his roommates worked in the Lieutenant Governor's Office. One night, this roommate came home from work and informed them that extradition papers had arrived that day, requesting that Ted be transferred from Utah to Colorado to stand trial for the murder of a woman named Caryn Campbell, and this transfer would take place in the early morning hours of January 28, 1977. He said, "We have had Ted all wrong. He isn't the man we thought he was. We need to change our opinion of him. Colorado has *real* evidence against Ted." He then told them about new evidence of pubic hair that had been found in Bundy's VW (and hair from the head of Carol DaRonch), which had been recovered from Ted's car after Colorado Investigator Mike Fisher had it delivered from Utah to the CBI (Colorado Bureau of Investigation) for further testing. Furthermore, he added, the transfer papers for Bundy's extradition from Utah to Colorado to stand trial for the murder of Caryn Campbell had come through and he was being prepared for transfer.

After hearing that investigators had tracked Bundy's gas purchases to locations at or near to where young women had disappeared--in this case, in Colorado--and at the same times they disappeared, the evidence was irrefutable. "This was real hard on us." Homer said. "We had been sure that Ted had been convicted on circumstantial evidence, that they had the wrong guy, that he was truly innocent. But now we were confronted with hard evidence that we couldn't deny. We started to question how we could have been fooled and why we didn't pick up some hint of the real Ted as we had interacted with him. Even looking back, few of us remembered anything that was out of place."

All of this came as a shock; an emotional bolt of lightning that scorched the reality of what Ted Bundy was and had been while they interacted with him. Without question they'd been deceived and betrayed by the man they all had counted as a friend. And they would not be the last to eventually feel betrayed by Ted Bundy.

Larry Anderson knew Bundy as well as anyone, and perhaps better than most of the other men in the Salt Lake City house. His remembrances of Ted Bundy are both stark and revealing. Like John Homer, Anderson found Bundy to be a very friendly person. And because Bundy was such a master of hiding his true diabolical nature from those who knew him, it was easy to do to his Utah friends what he'd done to his Washington friends.

Discussing Bundy with me over the phone recently, Anderson explained how normal Bundy seemed as he interacted with everyone. There was absolutely nothing on the surface that gave Larry Anderson, Wynn Bartholomew, John Homer, or anyone else in their house even the slightest degree of suspicion of Ted. Their relationships were progressing in a normal and stable fashion. Bundy had been seeking out members of the Mormon Church, was showing a clear interest in joining the church, and they extended their hand of fellowship to him.

And just as he had back home in Washington, Bundy was fitting right in with those in Utah. Anderson remembers Bundy being an excellent cook, and says that he introduced Ted to many girls who were members of the church and whom Bundy then dated. And, not surprisingly, there was never a single complaint from any of these young women with regard to Bundy's actions when they were out together. Indeed, Anderson and Bundy even double dated on more than one occasion.

But there were things that arose that Anderson would look back on *after* Bundy's arrest, and they were very telling. For example, after the attempted abduction of Carol DaRonch, a composite drawing of the attacker had been published in the local papers. One night while Bundy was at the house, the composite drawing was being passed around, and Bundy joined in the conversation. According to Anderson, as they were discussing how a person could pull off something like this, Bundy laughed and said, "I can tell you exactly how a person could do it," and then launched into how he'd worked with the governor of Washington, the time he spent on the Seattle Crime Commission, and how he learned about the various police jurisdictions, and how they don't always cooperate with each other. And then he uttered something that would become chillingly clear later on: "You could kidnap (a victim) from one location, kill in another, put the clothes (of the victim) in a different jurisdiction, the body in another, and none of it would be connected."

After the Chi Omega murders of January 1978 in Florida, Bundy would make a similar comment—a boast, really-- about the "unknown" Chi O killer to those at the rooming house when he lived on College Avenue in Tallahassee. He just couldn't shut his mouth.

Other incidents would stand out as well. Larry Anderson remembers when he and Ted planned a trip to Vail, Colorado, for some skiing in the winter months in early 1975. When the day arrived, Anderson was waiting for Bundy outside, packed with all his equipment and ready to go. But when Bundy showed up, he backed out of his commitment, saying, "Can I go by myself?" before quickly adding, "I need some time alone." Anderson remarked "I was waiting for him on the curb … He just drove up and canceled." Anderson noted that he would later learn the time of Bundy's "alone" trip coincided with one of the Colorado murders.

One day in October 1975, Anderson received a call from Bundy that at first he thought was a joke: "Anderson," Bundy began, "I've been arrested" (this would be his arrest for the abduction of Carol DaRonch). Then Ted blurted out,

"Look, I need some money or I'm going to get raped." As Anderson listened, Bundy explained what the "fix" should be: "Stick a couple twenties in your mouth and get them to me." Bundy assured him the money could be folded a certain way and placed in the side of the cheek and it wouldn't be discovered. Anderson, believing his friend was innocent, tried the implausible plan and it worked.

Sometime after Ted's conviction in the winter of 1976, Larry Anderson visited him at the Utah State Prison. They met in a maximum security room that was all steel (even the picnic-type table was metal), and Bundy told him he'd gotten into some trouble and that's why they were meeting in this particular room. He also immediately told Anderson, "Now, there's a camera and probably a microphone, so whisper." Bundy then launched into why he was in trouble: "Well, I got caught with some things in my possession, license and Social Security card."

Bundy then explained his plan to escape from prison, telling Anderson, "I want you to look around this room." Bundy then mentioned a vent that he believed he could crawl through that would lead him to the outside. He determined that he'd exit the yard at a location that would put him in a blind spot for the guards in the tower, which would aid him greatly in his plans. This is not to say that his plan would be successful, but the wheels in his head were turning and Ted Bundy was planning to escape. This meeting would be the last face-to-face encounter Larry Anderson would have with Ted Bundy.

One of the last things Larry told me was something that he and the others in Salt Lake City look back on with a bit of regret. When Bundy was charged with kidnapping Carol DaRonch, those who knew him didn't believe it was true. In their youthful ignorance they "knew" Bundy just had to be innocent. There just wasn't any way he could be guilty

65

of such an act; it couldn't be possible. (Bundy's friends in Washington echoed the same type of proclamation.) And so, knowing the police were following him while he was out on bail, they would sometimes drive Bundy (while presumably Bundy hid below the windows), to their house at 629 Eleventh Ave. where they would "slip him out the back basement backyard into a house that had a back entrance so he could come and go unseen. Of course we have no idea if the police were actually fooled by this." It was the least, they believed, they could do for a friend they sincerely believed had been wrongly accused.

Just as Bundy was busy trying to avoid the police, others were contacting the police about him. Back in Washington, his friend and former co-worker Ann Rule had been in contact with the Seattle cops about Ted, and at 10:50 a.m., on December 22, 1975, she put in a call to Seattle Police Capt. Nick Mackie with information she believed was pertinent to the ongoing case. Bundy was back in the area (he returned to Seattle in late November), after having made bail in Salt Lake City awaiting the upcoming trial in early 1976, and he called her earlier that morning complaining about the Seattle Police Department.

Rule told Detective Roger Dunn: "He said that he was upset because of the surveillance and the fact that they were talking to Liz again. He wants the tail stopped and claims it is because the cops don't know him like the cops in Utah, because he hasn't had any trouble with them since he's been down there. He said that he had seven lawyers working on his various cases." Rule also said Bundy told her "he would like to talk with Mackie to try to clear the air."

And then Rule repeated something Bundy said to her that "sounded peculiar": "If I did do it, I'm smart enough not to do anything else while I'm on trial."

Bundy's time back home in Washington would be

tumultuous for him. He was unnerved by all the public attention to his murders from the police, and the pressure this put on the killer had its intended effect: Bundy did not murder any young women while he was home in Washington.

Visiting Utah today, the state abounds with locations related to Bundy, although some sites have changed somewhat over the years. My original research trip to Utah occurred in 2006 in preparation for my first book on the case. During that visit I interviewed retired Detective Jerry Thompson and visited all of the pertinent locations regarding the case. My biggest surprise was the Fashion Place Mall in Murray: From the outside, it looked almost identical upon my arrival in 2006 to its appearance in 1974.

There is an excellent photograph of the mall taken after 1974 that appears in the 1992 Time-Life Books series *True Crime (Serial Killers),* and it would be in this same location that I would snap a photograph for *The Bundy Murders.* However, when we returned in 2015, everything had changed on this side of the mall. So much so, I at first believed we were at the wrong location. In 2006, Sears was still in the same location (as it was in 1974), as was See's Candies where Bundy encountered Carol DaRonch. Both Sears and See's Candies have moved on to other locations, and as far as the Bundy/DaRonch encounter, this side of the mall is now completely unrecognizable.

It was at this suburban mall that Bundy would have his first serious setback as an abductor, one that would have serious repercussions for him. Having scoped out the mall itself and the many patrons going to and fro, the killer spotted a very pretty woman with dark hair parted in the middle-- Carol DaRonch. Not only did he watch her park her car, but his eyes followed her into the mall. Keeping a safe distance from her, he watched her visit stores and then stop to speak with some people in the hallway between See's Candies and Waldenbooks. Once the conversation ended, Bundy made his move.

After introducing himself to Carol as "Officer Roseland," he informed her that someone had attempted to break into her car. Not suspecting anything nefarious out of the "well-attired" (as she told detectives) and handsome man, she followed him to her car. Of course, nothing looked out of place, and the car was locked. Even so, Bundy asked her to open the door of her car to make sure everything was okay, and she did so. And, just as it had looked when she just bent down and looked through the window, everything was fine. But Bundy didn't stop with that one request. He then asked her to open the passenger door, but Carol, who could easily be intimidated by authority figures, told him no. And while we cannot know for sure, it is likely Bundy had plans to have her slip into the car, and once inside, he would waylay her.

From here Bundy told her that his "partner" was inside the mall holding the suspect, and so the pair returned to the busy halls of the Fashion Place Mall. Not finding his partner, he told Carol they needed to go to a Murray police substation that was located across the side street on the other side of the mall. This substation was inside the cleaners and laundromat building, but when they reached the side door of the building, it was locked. Of course, Bundy knew it would be locked, and so this gave him the perfect excuse to tell Carol that they needed to drive the short distance to the main Murray police station, and she reluctantly agreed. But there would be no trip to the Murray P.D. in Bundy's plans.

If you walk through the mall and continue out the opposite doors, as "Officer Roseland" did with Carol DaRonch on that cool and drizzly November evening, it appears much the same, although the anchor store at this end is not what was here then. The "police substation" Bundy walked her to across the side street was actually the aforementioned cleaners and laundromat in 1974 and through at least my visit in 2006, but is now out of business and the property is vacant. This is also near to where (20 to 30 feet away) Bundy parked his VW, and where he convinced Carol DaRonch to enter his car so he could drive her, he said, to the main Murray police station where she could file a report.

But instead of heading to State Street, Bundy made a U-turn and drove half a block, turned left, and within one minute, stopped in front of the McMillan Elementary School at 315 E. 5900 S. and attacked Carol. She escaped from her captor after a brief but intense struggle (fighting in the darkness, she could feel, rather than see, the crowbar in Bundy's hand) and lived to tell the tale.

After the woman who ran screaming from his car was almost immediately picked up by an older couple, Bundy sped off into the night and within minutes, entered the on-ramp for Interstate-15 and headed north for Bountiful.

Today, if you visit the McMillan School, it still serves elementary students, and the building and surroundings look much the same as they did in 1974. Both times I've been there the weather was perfect, and I wondered, as the traffic passed by without taking notice of my actions, just how many people realize the horrific event that occurred there 41years ago. I found myself standing there imagining what it must have been like as he and Carol DaRonch fought in his little tan VW. He was bushy-haired at the time, as revealed in photographs, and she was a beautiful brunette he couldn't wait to kill. Knowing the story as described by Carol to police, it was easy to visualize the life-or-death struggle that took place here.

Once Bundy exited I-15 at Bountiful, he headed straight to Viewmont High School where a play, *The Red Head,* was getting ready to start. Bundy was able to focus in on this

school event because he'd picked up a flier for the play (no
doubt from a small bundle dropped off by the school) at the
Bountiful Recreational Center only two weeks before. Some
authors who write about Bundy believe he didn't actually
have a flier, that perhaps he saw a poster for it at the center.
This however is unlikely for two reasons: Unless he had
jotted down the information while there, he may not have
remembered all the particulars of when, where, and exactly
where the "where" was. And perhaps the most important
reason is that retired Detective Jerry Thompson told me
about the flier in 2005 when we first met, and it's something
he repeated again in 2006, and again in 2007 during a phone
call about another matter pertaining to the Debra Kent
abduction. There is no doubt in my mind Bundy had the
actual flier.

My first visit to Viewmont High was also in 2006, and
at that time I was allowed to photograph both the inside and
outside of the school. Very little has changed at Viewmont
with respect to the front of the building, the theater, and the
surrounding hallways and corridors. Some new construction
has occurred on the western side of the parking lot (where
Bundy had parked, as well as the Kents) and additional
construction towards the rear of the building has taken place
too, but that's about it. Anyone who had been there in 1974
would find the school today looking much the same. Bundy
would recognize it immediately.

In my book, I mention that at the time Debra Kent was
leaving the school prior to the end of the play to pick up her
brother at a roller skating rink, someone reported hearing
one or two screams of a female coming from the parking lot
of Viewmont High. Someone also spotted a VW speeding
away from the school at about the same time. There were,
in fact, numerous individuals who heard both a scream or
screams and a loud bang. What follows is taken directly

from a Colorado court document titled "Offer of Proof of Similar Transactions":

"The evidence will show that Mr. Orval Ryver, 1195 North 200 West, Bountiful, Utah, heard a girl scream several times very loudly at approximately 10:55 p.m. on November 8, 1974, as he was arriving home from work. Mr. Ryver's testimony would indicate that the screams sounded kind of desperate. The evidence will also indicate that he saw the lights of a midsize car leaving the west driveway of Viewmont High School.

"The evidence will indicate that Linda J. Olson of 154 West 10th North, a location also near the Viewmont High School, heard three very loud screams which she described as a girl's voice which sounded as though she was really scared at approximately 10:20 p.m. on November 8, 1974.

"Evidence will indicate that Steve Lakin, 971 North Chapel Drive # 4, heard a loud explosion which came from the front of Viewmont High School at approximately 10:45 a.m. on November 8, 1974, and that at approximately 11:00 p.m. he heard screams coming from the Viewmont area. Mr. Larkin left his apartment to investigate this incident and went to Viewmont because he thought someone was really in trouble.

"Further evidence will indicate that Mr. George L. Bates, 997 North Chapel Drive # 6, heard a girl yell or scream which to him sounded rather bad at approximately 10:30 p.m. on November 8, 1974.

"Further evidence will indicate that Mr. and Mrs. Portrey, 971 North Chapel Drive # 2, were at their residence and heard a loud bang and a girl scream at a time between 10:45 p.m. and 11:15 p.m. on November 8, 1974.

"Evidence will also indicate that a Linda Larkin, 971 Chapel Drive # 4, heard a blast or pop and a girl scream at approximately 10:55 p.m. on November 8, 1974.

"The evidence will show that there are other witnesses in addition to those already mentioned who heard a bang and heard a girl's screams at time between 10:30 p.m. and 11:00 p.m. on November 8, 1974."

It is of interest to note that "bangs" were heard the night of the abduction, and we're left to wonder exactly from where these sounds originated. Did Bundy swing his crowbar at Debra Kent and miss, only to strike a car (which would also have given her time to scream), or was it something else producing this sound? Carol DaRonch testified that Bundy had a pistol on the night he abducted her, and that she struggled with him in the VW as he tried to hit her with the crowbar. Did Bundy actually have a pistol that evening? If he did, it would be a bit unusual, in my view, and Bundy never mentioned a gun, nor did anybody ever see him with one (I was also told by someone very close to the DaRonch case that there were doubts among the prosecutors that a handgun was ever involved). And yet, if it wasn't the crowbar crashing into a parked car, could it have been a small caliber handgun making that "pop" or "bang" referred to in the above interviews? We may never know.

Being late at night, with limited lighting in the parking lot, Bundy had the perfect environment in which to attempt another murder. Since the play had not yet ended, Bundy and Debra Kent were the only ones in the lot, and Bundy would accomplish his goal very quickly. That so many people heard her scream is amazing, given the distance from where killer and victim would have been standing to the apartments across the street or the houses adjacent to the school.

And, once again, the killer fled with his victim into the night.

Another interesting back story to a Utah murder is related to the killing of Laura Aime. When I wrote *The Bundy*

Murders, I stuck to the story that Bundy did not know Aime prior to her death, and this in fact may be the case (Bundy told Florida detectives that he never harmed anyone that he knew). That said, these stories have circulated in some of the Bundy books, and so I will reproduce from the record that which has been told by some who knew Aime. What follows is again taken from the Colorado court document titled "Offer of Proof of Similar Transactions":

"There will be testimony that Theodore Robert Bundy knew Laura Ann Aime and they had talked on several occasions. Witnesses will testify that Ted Bundy hung around Brown's Café, which was frequented also by Laura Ann Aime. Bundy drank coffee and flirted with the girls. Ted Bundy occasionally sat with Laura Ann Aime and her girlfriends. On one occasion when Laura Ann Aime was about to leave, Ted Bundy blocked her in a booth and stated 'You can't go, I'm going to rape you'; a witness to that, will testify that Laura Ann Aime shoved him out of the booth and left. This occurred in late summer or early fall of 1974. On another occasion, in late September or early October, Laura Ann Aime introduced Ted Bundy to a group of her friends, including Jim Stone (a pseudonym). Jim Stone and Ted Bundy got into an argument after Jim puts grass in Laura's halter top. Bundy told Jim to leave Laura alone because Laura was his girl. Laura told Bundy to 'get screwed.' Bundy was left speechless."

This does make for interesting reading, to be sure. But if you've read my first book on Ted Bundy you know it didn't make the cut. It's not that I think this story can't be true, because it may very well be true. But it did not feel right to me the first few times I read it in 2007, and it doesn't feel good now. In other words, there's a big question mark hanging over it all, and it is for this reason I have left it out entirely the first time around. Still, it's interesting to contemplate.

The final piece of the Laura Aime connection has to do with my late friend James Massie, who originally introduced me to Jerry Thompson, for without Jim's introduction, *The Bundy Murders* would never have been written, and you wouldn't be reading these words either. Anyway, in the early 1980s, Jim traveled to Utah to conduct research and meet some of the families of the victims and others involved in the case. I believe it was at this time that he was introduced to Detective Jerry Thompson and Dr. Al Carlisle.

One of the families Jim grew close to was the Aime family and especially to Jim Aime. The two men got along well, and as can be expected, his grief was just under the surface of his personality. One day as the two men were driving past the spot where Laura had been found, Jim Aime blurted out, "My little baby was up there all by herself and there was nothing I could do to help her." Jim Massie also believed that Jim Aime passed away well before his time due to his daughter's murder and the distress that he suffered because of her death.

Bundy would go on to murder others in Utah. It was maddening for authorities to have a killer of young women on the loose and not be able to stop him. It was, in fact, the same scenario that Washington detectives were forced to endure only months earlier (and they were still searching for the killer). But this killer of women was good at what he did, and he benefited from an extraordinary long streak of good luck. No matter how bizarre his abductions became (Lynda Ann Healy, Denise Naslund and Janice Ott, and Debra Kent), he would elude his pursuers until 1975.

Indeed, the police activity on the killer's trail by the end of 1974 became so heavy in Utah that Bundy decided to branch out to Colorado in the first month of 1975. It was time to find a new killing ground, and Bundy couldn't wait to spread the horror there.

CHAPTER THREE
New Killing Grounds: 1975

Theodore Bundy, being the homicidal entity that he had become, set out for the Colorado ski resorts in early 1975. By this time he fully understood that he'd turned Utah into the same investigative nightmare for himself that he'd created in Washington. As a result, women in nearby Colorado were going to die, and the first one to fall victim in that state (that we know of) was pretty Caryn Campbell of Michigan (for a more complete, detailed story of this murder, and all the murders I mention in this book, see my 2009 best-seller, *The Bundy Murders: A Comprehensive History*).

On the bitter cold evening of January 12, 1975, Bundy was standing next to an outdoor service closet and across from an elevator at the very popular Wildwood Inn, in Snowmass Village. He certainly wasn't dressed for it, as he was wearing dress slacks and a shirt. His appearance looked so odd that Elizabeth Harter noticed him and immediately wondered why he would be doing such a thing. He stood out, she later told police investigators, and she thought it was weird.

What brought Bundy to this particular distant location (from Salt Lake City), and why did he stop at this particular ski resort? No one knows. It would be there, at this tiny crossroads of a service closet, an elevator, and a small second-floor walkway, that he would encounter twenty-three-year-old Caryn Campbell, a nurse from Michigan. And by some ruse, he'd convince her to follow him to his car in one of the adjoining parking lots, where he knocked her unconscious.

After he placed Caryn inside his VW (most likely with the passenger seat already removed), he drove to a spot on Owl Creek Road, approximately 2.8 miles from the inn, where he sexually assaulted and murdered her. Later, he would tell Mike Fisher, the chief investigator for the Pitkin County Attorney's Office in Aspen, that "I did my thing right there in the car." His "thing," of course, was to have sex with his victims from behind (either vaginal or anal) and choke them to death with an electrical cord (usually) or a rope (occasionally). But a deeper look into the actual abduction of Caryn Campbell is necessary.

It is of interest to note that, as Bundy braced against the wind and extreme cold on the second-floor balcony that night, only one floor below him was an open air and very popular swimming pool, a pool that was in use at the same time he was waiting for the perfect victim to emerge from the elevator. But that wouldn't have concerned him at all. Being a heated pool, vast amounts of steam were constantly wafting off the surface of the water, and this created a type of screen, if you will, where people could often hear the voices of those walking by, while they remained hidden by the mist.

Add to this his hiding on the second floor, and you have an almost perfect concealment from the public. And Bundy, who never missed an opportunity to use such things to his advantage for his diabolical purposes, would not have been ignorant of this.

When Mike Fisher and I were exchanging many emails during 2007 and 2008 (along with the occasional phone calls), I received a tremendous amount of vital information regarding Ted Bundy, the Colorado murders, and the case in general. In the midst of all this, Mike also provided the interesting story of the only person to see Ted Bundy at the Wildwood Inn, someone who must have seen him only moments before he coaxed Caryn Campbell to follow him to where he attacked her.

A Dr. Parker (a pseudonym) was among those originally interviewed by Fisher in 1975. When the detective returned to the inn one year later to speak again with those who'd returned for the new skiing season, Fisher learned something new and vital from the doctor. This new information had to do with a woman named Elizabeth Harter, whom Fisher had also met in 1975 but from whom he received nothing of substance. However, Elizabeth Harter had, merely in passing, mentioned to Dr. Parker that she had encountered a strange man at the elevator around the time Caryn Campbell disappeared. Here, in Fisher's own words, is the story. For clarity, it appears in italics:

I learned that Dr. Parker and Mrs. Harter were to be at the Wildwood Inn again in January of 1976, one year after Caryn's disappearance. Mrs. Harter was not of interest to me at the time since she was sick while here in 1975. Dr. Parker was my target, he might be able to ID, the missing Michael (Michael was a supposed employee of the Inn that Dr. Parker had seen in the pool that night)....was Theodore. He had nixed other persons of interest when I had their photographs sent to California for him to see. I met with Dr. Parker in the same room at the Wildwood Inn he occupied in 1975. He was very polite, and I as entered his room, he pointed to the people that I was back, the persistent investigator in Colorado he said, (and) there sat Mrs. Harter and her family. We exchanged pleasantries. Dr. Parker excused himself and partially closed the adjoining room door. We pulled up a couple chairs and faced the bed and I explained that I was still investigating the disappearance of the lady and I wanted him to look at photographs in an effort to determine if any of the people in the photos were the "Michael" he saw in the pool.

The doctor took his time, and with responsible interest he went through the photos looking at them closely. I had several photos and only two that depicted Theodore Bundy; one was the lineup and the other his booking photo at the Salt Lake County Jail. For the lineup photo Theodore had changed the way he combed his hair (and he also had cut his hair the day before). With some exasperation he sat back into the chair and said, "No" I don't see that "Michael" among any of the photos. He compliments me on being persistent, and encourages me stick with it. Looking me straight in the face he said, you should take the time to show those photos to Mrs. Harter, (as) she told us after we left in 1975 of a strange man that she saw here at the inn just before meeting you last year. I asked him "What man, she never mentioned seeing a strange man to me, only that she was sick," the kind doctor replied that "she's mentioned him several times to us (meaning their group) when we talk of the vacation season."

I was stunned! Dr. Parker and I walked to the adjoining room door, he opened it and I asked Mrs. Harter if she would mind talking with me for a few moments. She came into room I closed the door and asked her to tell me about their last stay there in 1975, she repeated that their trip to Mexico had gone bad when they all came down with diarrhea, her husband was the sickest and her daughter recovered more quickly. They had not been able to ski.

She continued to tell me that on the evening the lady disappeared from the hotel she had to go for some soup for her husband. It was so very cold, and she was hurrying to get the soup and get back to the warmth of the room. She had to go to the village to get the soup, and she walked north along the east side of the hotel walkway and down the stairs and across the street, order the soup and then walk back to their room. Walking north along the walkway she came to the pillar that is across from the elevator, there, next to the ski lockers, was this "strange man," she said. I asked her to define "strange" and she told me that everyone due to the cold that season and that it was a ski resort was dressed in ski clothing or warm clothing, what made the man strange was that he wasn't wearing any skiing or warm clothing, no boots, no scarf, light pants, no gloves, he didn't have skis with him and he was just standing there doing nothing. He startled her, he was standing back out of the light to the east of the elevator (that would have been on Caryn's left as she got out of the elevator, and her attention was directed to the west, or her right toward her room.)

She didn't tell anyone of the strange man until they had returned to California and felt better and she had mentioned him to her husband and Dr. Parker on a number of occasions, she opinioned that was why Dr. Parker mentioned it to me, she hadn't expected him to do that. I asked Mrs. Harter if she could remember him well enough to give me a description and she supplied a very good description of him, and his clothing. According to Mrs. Harter she could identify him again...I laid out the photos over the same bed that I had used when interviewing Dr Parker. She looked over the batch of photos and picked up the line up photo and held it, then she picked up the booking photos of Theodore and continued looking over the photos, then she looked at the photos she picked up and told me that, pointing to Theodore in the lineup photo that that was the strange man she had seen next to the elevator. I asked if she was sure, she said yes she was. I had her initial each photo that she identified and date them. I asked if she knew any of the other people depicted in the photos still laying on the bed, she looked for a few moments and told me "no." I had Mrs. Harter walk me through her entire walk for the soup, she was adamant about the strange man and where he stood, and how he looked, she didn't like him she said. I returned to the room with Mrs. Harter and thanked them all for the time apologizing for the interruption of their day.

When Mrs. Harter picked Theodore's photo up I didn't know what to do, screaming and hugging Mrs. Harter had come to mind, I was nervous and cautious with everything I said to her after that moment. I wanted to cry out to the world, that I knew what had happened, I'd been correct – at last. When I got in the car my emotions had escalated ecstatic level, I just sat there with the keys to my car in my hand. All the work, the bitter cold nights, the constant interviews, and those huge disappointments had just been justified. But I knew it wasn't over yet, there was a long way to go. And a great disappointment was laying in wait for me.

That disappointment came in the form of Elizabeth Harter's failure to identify Bundy in court during the trial. Although she had no trouble matching the photographs of Bundy to the man she saw in the elevator, she failed to identify him in court. This struck Fisher as strange, and he has firm opinions as to why this happened, and it's more than plausible, but because it's speculation, I will not be adding this to the book.

Today, the Wildwood Inn looks much the same as it did on that tragic evening. The name "Wildwood Inn" remains on the outer wall of this iconic winter resort, but it has changed owners several times since the 1970s, and is in fact today a Holiday Inn Express. When we arrived at the inn, we parked in the lot (the lot itself was actually flat in this otherwise steep location) that is to the right of the main entrance. As my wife and I crossed the street I actually had to lean to my right a bit just to keep my equilibrium, and I in fact, imagined that someone, at some point in the past, easily could have fallen and rolled like a log down this exceedingly steep hill.

As you enter the front door, you are looking straight at the elevator that Caryn Campbell took that night to retrieve the magazine from her room. Off to the left is the sunken bar and lounging area with the fireplace situated in the center of the room. It was here that Dr. Raymond Gadowski, Caryn's boyfriend, waited with his two children as they warmed themselves around the fire, but Caryn never returned.

I want to mention too that it's impossible (for me, anyway), to visit any of these sites without having a sense of what happened at these places. It happened when I visited the rooming house of Lynda Ann Healy in Seattle, or Lake Sammamish, or other locations as well. For me, the Wildwood Inn means Ted Bundy and the murder of the now forever-young Caryn Campbell, and nothing more. So being here, or at any other Bundy murder, abduction, or burial site, is like entering another world and another time. At that moment I'm seeing everything through the kaleidoscope of the events of the Ted Bundy murders. Others come and go here, and for most of them, the hotel's infamous history is unknown.

One of the most remarkable examples of this is when I was attempting to locate Bundy's 565 First Ave. rooming residence in Salt Lake City for the first time. I had never been on the street before, and as we drove down First Avenue I was looking for the address, and as we were slowing down, I had this strange sense of oppression, or something negative, coming from a house that was sitting behind, and being obscured by, two trees. As the car crept past the trees, the house I'd seen in photographs from the 1970s came into view. Above the front door were the numbers 565. We were now there.

I remember thinking how odd it was that this house, once the home of America's premier serial killer (Bundy actually kept several of his victims alive and inside the residence), was somehow still emitting a bit of that dark energy that once lived and moved within its walls.

Bundy would continue to kill in Colorado. He would snatch Julie Cunningham from Vail, Denise Oliverson from Grand Junction, and others would die by his hand as well. But it would not just be Colorado that would suffer in 1975.

Myth vs. Fact in the Lynette Culver Abduction

On May 5, 1975, Bundy would journey to Pocatello, Idaho, to hunt college-aged women, but he would come up empty-handed during his hunt on the first day and evening. The weather played a part in thwarting him as it was cold that May, and snow showers blanketed the city during this time. Convincing women to stop and talk with him, or follow him, just wasn't going to happen. He was also "chased" out of a woman's high-rise dormitory on the college campus, and these failures may have caused Bundy to change tactics the next day. Unable to snatch a woman, Bundy would capture a girl, which leads us to this:

When I was conducting research for my book *The Bundy Murders*, I discovered new and previously unpublished information on the abduction and murder of twelve-year-old

Lynette Culver of Pocatello. Not only that, but I learned a great deal about Bundy's two-day odyssey to that location. Not only was I able to obtain the police case file and the end-of-life confession transcript Bundy gave two days prior to his execution, but I was very fortunate to have the corroboration of Russ Reneau and Randy Everitt of the Idaho Attorney General's Office. Although I dealt mostly with Russ through telephone conversations and emails, I finally caught up with Randy by phone one night, and I'm very thankful for the information provided by these two men. Having the official record of the Lynette Culver abduction was great, but having the remembrances of these two very capable investigators to go along with it was invaluable.

To give you, the reader, a background on this murder, and how little was known about it (excluding the investigators, of course), I'll give a brief summary of what was out there in books prior to the publication of *The Bundy Murders*. Although I will not name any particular Bundy book, I will recount what was already out there as I was conducting my research.

One very popular book has Bundy driving to Pocatello, committing the murder, and returning the same day. Apparently, another popular Bundy book mentions the actual (and accurate) method Bundy used to kill Lynette, but it disappears in later editions. Not one of the books goes into great detail about both the abduction and murder, and most references to the killing of Lynette Culver mention the murder only and that's all. Early on I determined that I would leave no proverbial stone unturned when searching for the truth, and that I would find all that I could find about each of the murders, and this included the case of Lynette Culver. Of course, I had no idea how different my road would become as I searched for the truth for this particular case, but I soon found out.

When I started writing the book, I covered all the murders sequentially. I didn't gather all the material sequentially, as I was gathering case files from various states sometimes at the same time. But when it came to writing the story of the Bundy murders, I began with his birth, his childhood, and where he began his career of murder, in Washington state. And so, it was a while before I came to the murder of Lynette, and she was the only victim in which I did not have (at that time) a case file. And so, I asked the former Colorado investigator, Mike Fisher, about her, just in a passing conversation. And Mike informed me that Bundy had drowned the girl in a bathtub at the Holiday Inn in Pocatello.

At the time Mike mentioned this I gave it little thought. But I soon decided I should make a call to Bill Hagmaier, the former FBI agent who was, during the Bundy years, a part of the Behavioral Science Unit, to see what if anything he knew about Lynette Culver's death. I had already made at least one phone call to Bill prior to this, so it wasn't a cold call and that was good. Anyway, I asked him about the girl, stating that outside of her name and the manner of her death, I didn't know anything else about her. What I didn't yet realize was the manner of death of young Lynette was about to become a sticking point. Bill said that while he had a great deal of respect for the detective who gave me this information (he and Mike Fisher liked one another), he'd never heard a story that Bundy had drowned the girl in a bathtub, and he also mentioned that such a method of killing would not follow Bundy's MO of killing girls while having sex with them from behind and strangling them. Furthermore, he said, he'd sat in on every confession at the end of Bundy's life, and had never heard anything like that. He did, however, ask me to let him know if I learned any additional information about it, and I assured him that I would.

Picking up the phone, I telephoned Mike Fisher and told

him of Hagmaier's reaction. He, in turn, said I needed to contact Russ Reneau, who received this information directly from Bundy. Mike also mentioned that Russ had passed this information along to him when they were still in Florida just prior to Bundy's execution. I must admit, by this time I was scratching my head and wondering if what I'd been told was true. After all, I reasoned, Hagmaier was the expert with respect to knowledge of Bundy and the case in general, as he had sat in on every confession, and I was but the novice researcher. And in the back of my mind, I believed Hagmaier could be right after all.

Tracking down Russ Reneau was not too difficult (I'd grown accustomed by this time to tracking down otherwise hard to find people). And I must add that when I first spoke to Russ, he was like all the investigators I'd met thus far: friendly, open, and willing to share with me the story of Bundy's foray into Idaho, and the facts behind the Lynette Culver murder. And when you need facts–what's true and what's not–there's no better place to go than the original investigators.

My first question, of course, was the manner in which Lynette Culver had been killed, adding that I'd been told Bundy drowned her in the bathtub. Reneau immediately confirmed that what Mike Fisher had told me was true, and he explained why Bill Hagmaier didn't know about it.

The interview during which Bundy brought the girl up lasted exactly one hour and was held in a room with a partition of glass separating Bundy from Russ Reneau, his co-investigator Randy Everitt, Bundy's attorney Diana Weiner, and FBI Agent Bill Hagmaier. As their time with Bundy couldn't exceed one hour, the questions were quick-paced and jumped back and forth between the two murders linked to Bundy in the state: the hitchhiker he said he picked up and murdered on his way to Utah in September 1974, and the murder of Lynette Culver.

At some point in the interview, Bundy mentions Lynette's manner of death as drowning, and because he said he'd placed her in a river "north of Pocatello" the investigators assumed the drowning occurred there. However, because Bundy hadn't stated emphatically that she drowned in the river, Reneau asked Everitt to return to the prison and ask Bundy about it. (Bundy had told investigators when the original interview came to an end, that he would give them additional information if they needed it.)

Perhaps to Everitt's surprise, authorities allowed him to re-enter the prison and guards escorted him to a room. In about 20 minutes, Bundy was led into the room and sat down with Everitt. When asked about the drowning, Bundy said he had drowned the girl in the bathtub, and Reneau told me that Bundy also admitted to having sex with the girl's body after she was dead. Technically, this meeting shouldn't have occurred at all, as Bundy's attorney wasn't present, and Hagmaier was absent as well. Soon after learning this, I emailed Bill Hagmaier, and here is a portion of that email dated April 5, 2007:

Hi Bill--

Well, the mystery is solved. Bundy did in fact drown the Culver girl in the Holiday Inn bathtub. Since we last spoke over the phone, I've received the transcript of Bundy's confession from the Idaho Atty. Gen's office. In the transcript Bundy admits drowning her, but doesn't give any details concerning where or how this was done. So this is why Russ sent Randall back to the prison. I have since confirmed, (I spoke to Randall today by phone) that he received the additional information about the bathtub from a face-to-face meeting with Ted.

I was happy I had finally gotten to the truth behind the murder of Lynette Culver. But what came out of my research was far more than this, as I was able to piece together Bundy's activities during his two-day stay in the city and how the continuing wintry weather (in May) played a part in his inability to snatch a college coed on his first day of hunting (the full story of Bundy's trip to Pocatello can be found in my book, *The Bundy Murders*, Pages 136-139). Bundy would encounter Lynette at her school around lunch time on the second day. And now we must confront a myth about the murder of Lynette that has been repeated for many years.

According to this urban legend, Lynette Culver left Alameda Middle School (identified as a junior high school in police records of the time; and, oddly, listed as such today), and was "seen" boarding a bus. Other "sightings" have her walking near another school a couple of blocks away around 2:30 p.m. (according to Bundy, she was dead, already being transported, and being placed in the river by 3:00 p.m.). Of course, when I was writing my first book about Bundy, and telling of his meandering his way from the Holiday Inn, on a practically straight shot from his hotel, until he came to Alameda Middle School, where he picked up the doomed girl, I was already aware of the false sightings given to police in the first few days after her abduction. These "sightings" reports are almost always well-meaning, but they do nothing for the investigation. And the later ramifications of such worthless rabbit trails, is that they will lead future researchers down the wrong path. Fortunately for me in writing about the case after the fact, I had the entire police record, Bundy's invaluable confession transcript, and the friendly ear of retired Investigator Russ Reneau.

Speaking of it recently by phone, Reneau said there's no truth to accounts that Bundy had encountered Lynette Culver anywhere *other than* Alameda Middle School. He said that such statements "go against what Bundy told us." It was a myth, and Russ Reneau knew it.

And finally, a word about eyewitness reports and statements: In my original files of the Bundy murders, I have numerous pages, filled with the statements of well-meaning people who absolutely believed they'd seen some of the missing women in other locations (and in some cases, other states), and every one of these "leads" had to be investigated. And yet, not one tip given to authorities was true. All of the girls were dead, and some long dead. The truth is that by 2:30 that afternoon of May 6, 1975, preteen Lynette Culver was either dead, in the process of dying, or soon would be. She was in the hands of a lethal entity, and there would be no escape.

The rear portion of the Holiday Inn (now the Clarion)
in Pocatello, Idaho, where Bundy took young Lynette
Culver and drown her in the bathtub.

Visiting Pocatello today, you'll find many sites looking much the same as they did when Ted Bundy came to town. Alameda Middle School appears to be identical to what it looked like when Bundy rolled his VW up to the school. Across the street from the school (to its side) is Fairbanks Avenue, the street Lynette Culver lived on. Because of a typographical error on one of the police reports, her address was listed as "23 Fairbanks Avenue." It was long after *The Bundy Murders* went to press that I discovered the typo and that the actual address was 231 Fairbanks. So when we visited the city during our summer 2015 trip, I was determined to get a picture of her house. However, I soon discovered that all the Fairbanks addresses were changed a number of years ago, and because of this, I could not identify the former Culver home.

During my October 2015 telephone call to Russ Reneau, I asked him about Bundy's demeanor and attitude while they were there, and whether Bundy had looked at him eye-to-eye. He said Bundy was very tired, and that he did look them in the eyes while talking about things in a general sense. But as he described the murders, he would look away, as if he were concentrating. He also said that as Bundy talked about the abduction and murder of Lynette Culver, he became noticeably focused on what he was saying. At the beginning of the interview, Bundy was the first one to speak. Although he seemed a bit disjointed, Russ said, it was clear he was ready to get down to business and make the confessions. What follows is the transcript of Bundy beginning the interview:

"All right, let's begin with…try to focus in on the date here…the period. I believe it's April 1975, possibly May. It's in one of those two months. I traveled from Salt Lake City to…now here is my confusion to either Pocatello or Idaho Falls and I tend to think it was Pocatello but I'm not absolutely sure. Trying to recall perhaps the day of the week…again I know it was during the week, not on a weekend. I stayed in a Holiday Inn in, well in all likelihood Pocatello…for at least one night. I'm cutting down on a lot of factual stuff right now…you're free to ask. Just to give you the picture. I abducted a young girl from a junior high school, probably in Pocatello."

Today, the Holiday Inn in Pocatello is the Clarion Hotel, still located at 1399 Bench Road. It's had a number of names over the years, but the layout of the hotel remains the same. Bundy, thinking ahead and desiring secrecy, chose a room in the rear of the building. What's interesting about the back of the structure is that it snakes around the property and is anything but a straight line. When I visited the site to take photographs it was impossible to get it all in with one shot because of the angles (I also narrated a video about the hotel for the blog of my publisher, WildBlue Press), and we have only a close approximation of where the actual room was located. What follows is from Bundy, taken directly from the transcript during his end-of-life interview with Idaho investigators:

"Reneau: Do you know what part of the Holiday Inn you were staying in?

"Bundy: Yes.

"Reneau: Can you describe for me from the entrance approximately where your room would have been?

"Bundy: It was all the way around the what I would call the back, the far side from the desk, the main entrance then all the around the back side, so you drive basically all the way around to the back. You know you'd have to take a circuitous route around the, the various wings of the Holiday Inn to get around to the back side of it, and it would've been on the first floor, I mean the ground level."

Bundy ended the hour in a conciliatory mood: "See what you...you know, I don't need to tell you your job but if you come up with questions that are important...that you simply want me to answer...perhaps I can find a way to do that. I know this isn't much time."

And this is exactly what he did when Randy Everitt interviewed him for the second time that day, learning more about the abduction and killing of Lynette Culver.

Bundy would continue to kill after murdering the twelve-year-old girl in Pocatello. The homicidal maniac had thus far killed in Washington, Utah, Colorado, and Idaho, and authorities had no idea who was committing the slaughter. But that would change in the near future.

CHAPTER FOUR
The Unmasking

Bundy was hunting the night he was arrested. Without question, he was after a girl or young woman to kill. The passenger seat of his VW was pulled out and lying in the backseat so he'd have room to lay an unconscious victim on the floor of the car, and his murder kit was in full view, open, with some of the contents spilling out of the bag.

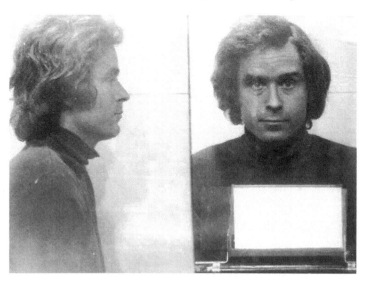

The beginning of the end: Ted Bundy's August 16, 1975 arrest in Granger, Utah (courtesy King County Archives)

Feeling impervious to detection, Bundy was nabbed by a Utah highway patrol officer in the small community of Granger, on August 15, 1975. He was sitting in his car in a darkened neighborhood smoking a joint and consulting a map because, he later told the cops, he was trying to figure out a way home. When he saw headlights zeroing in on him, he took off. Within moments he saw the red glow of a police cruiser's light bathing his car, and after speeding through the streets for a few minutes, he pulled over and was arrested. This began Bundy's slow unraveling. All those dark secrets of what he had done; secrets he had so carefully guarded would soon be known by everyone. Although this night brought only the charge of evading a police officer and possessing suspected burglary tools (he would be released hours later), Bundy had entered the Utah law enforcement sphere, and additional charges would soon be coming.

It would all take time, of course. But once the investigative ball began rolling, it would snowball, and Bundy was forced to watch it and there wasn't one thing he could do to stop it. By the fall of that year, Utah authorities would successfully link Bundy with the kidnapping of Carol DaRonch, and he would stand trial and be convicted of that crime in February 1976. In Colorado, Mike Fisher would, in the coming months, obtain a murder warrant against Bundy for the murder of Caryn Campbell who had been led away from the Wildwood Inn in Snowmass a year earlier. That murder warrant meant Bundy was going to stand trial in Aspen in 1977 and he would be escorted there personally by Mike Fisher and crew.

Once again, I will again be using vital information I received from Mike Fisher during my research for *The Bundy Murders*. Some of this material was presented (sometimes in quotes, sometimes in my own words) in my first book on the case, but other facts I'll be using for the first time. And indeed, for posterity's sake, I'll be quoting him verbatim for much of it. Some of this material will pertain to Utah as Fisher, of necessity, conducted his own investigation in that neighboring state so Colorado authorities could build a case against Ted Bundy using a legal term called "similar transactions."

Seeking to point out similar transactions in this case meant that, while Colorado was prosecuting Bundy for Caryn Campbell's murder, it was the desire of Fisher to show a pattern (Bundy's MO) between that killing in Colorado and other murders investigated in Utah. If this would have been allowed by the presiding judge (he ultimately disallowed them), any additional evidence that Fisher came up with in Utah could then be linked to present to the jury exactly what had happened wherever Bundy took up residence. This meant that Mike Fisher would be doing his own intense investigation into the Utah murders, and this would include interviewing many who were personally involved.

What follows is one of the many emails I received from Mike during the research for *The Bundy Murders*. Italics are used for clarity to distinguish the email from other text. I have also made minimal corrections for typos or the occasional misspelled name, and where delicate information was presented, it has been omitted to protect those involved:

Deputy District Attorney Milton K. Blakey had been on loan to our office from Colorado Springs. He was responsible for the entire prosecution of Theodore Bundy. As the investigation continued with only slight improvements, and after being made aware of the similarities of the Debra Kent disappearance, Melissa Smith's murder, Laura Ann Amie's murder and Theodore's arrest for kidnapping, Blakey decided that our case needed to include the similar transactions, as many as possible. He directed me to go back to Salt

Lake County and reinvestigate every one of those cases for presentation in Colorado. There would be pretrial hearings of an evidentiary nature to establish whether or not they could be used. After Theodore's arrest and the search of his VW bug we had Caryn Campbell's hair, and that of Melissa Smith. Hairs were found in the front and back seat, both head and pubic hair was found in Melissa's case.

After Theodore's conviction (in the DaRonch case) I traveled to Salt Lake City, Utah, and met with Det. Jerry Thompson, he made a complete copy of their case available. Jerry and I walked through the DaRonch kidnapping scene, I photograph the mall again and then began to interview everyone in the case again. We walked the mall and talked of Theodore's chosen route, it was out of sight, longer but easier for him to make a getaway if the abductions didn't work. DaRonch was suspicious of him driving a VW bug when he was supposed to be a police officer.

Theodore had been picked from a lineup by the daughter of a local FBI resident agent. She seemed to love the attention, she was attractive very warm and open with the detectives, and she made the identification. The procedure for the line was set down as Jerry and I talked, who else was in the lineup, mostly cops ... As I reviewed the paperwork associated with the lineup I noted that there were other witnesses at the lineup. The witnesses were just given a piece of paper and instructed to write down the number of anyone they knew, and then they'd be interviewed later. Thumbing through the witness slips I noticed that one of the other witnesses had written down that she knew the person in the line (by number). I asked who that person was; I didn't see any interview of that person. Jerry looked over all the witness listed, the other came from the Debra Kent case, they were people at the school play from where she disappeared, later in the evening of the DaRonch attempted kidnapping. Jerry referred to the file and told me that it was a girl who went to school with Debra. He didn't know where she was at. I asked about the follow-up interview and he told me that probably wasn't done by Salt Lake S/O, and since that was Bountiful, Utah's case they may have contacted her. There was no explanation for why she was not interviewed immediately.

At Bountiful PD I learned (that) Brenda Clark (a pseudonym); the missing lineup witness, was not interviewed in depth after the lineup or any other time... and was now living in the area. I told them I had to have her at the Bountiful Police Department. I met her in the afternoon, after finishing another interview. She was older looking and very quiet, very quiet. I brought her into the interview and sat for a while without talking. She appeared to be more comfortable, and I began the interview. Responding to questions she told that she knew she was there for Debra Kent. She had identified the man she saw in the auditorium of Viewmont High School the night that Debra disappeared. She told me that they asked a few questions about her identifying the lineup suspect. But they didn't follow up.

She slowly and methodically told me that she had seen the man in the lineup at the auditorium the night Debbie disappeared. She had noticed him standing behind where she was seated; he was leaning against a waist high wall [there is a picture of this wall in my book, The Bundy Murders] that separated the seats from the rear aisle ... She described him to a tee.

She sat and watched the play and kept an observant eye on the man in back. He would lean against the short wall, then step back and lean up against the auditorium wall...I asked about the distance between the man behind her, and Debra Kent. She told me that Debbie was sitting just a few rows ahead of her. Debbie knew she (Brenda) and her mother were there, they had acknowledged each other at the beginning of the performance with the Kents coming into the auditorium. I had Brenda draw a diagram of the auditorium area and where Debbie was seated and where she sat, and where the man stood. It was remarkable; she put Theodore within 15 feet of Debra Kent. Brenda continued telling me that Debra was very visible to the man in the back when she stood up as the play was finishing. When she looked at Debra mouthing goodnight, Debra was headed up the aisle and passing by her and going out the door. When she looked again, the man was gone.

Brenda was very soft spoken, but there was emotion in what she was saying, no tears, but watery eyes; an unsteadiness. I looked at her without saying anything, and then she went on-- Debra left the building before she did. She was silently tearful. I was stunned at what I had just learned. The prize witness for Debra Kent's disappearance was there all the time.

Without question, Mike Fisher was exceedingly pleased to locate someone who not only saw Bundy, but also knew Debra Kent and saw her that evening. It was excellent news in this long and protracted investigation.

Then there was the incident Fisher described in an email of the woman Bundy approached in the parking lot of Viewmont prior to his entering the theater that night:

We located the girl that had been approached by a man in the parking lot the night of Debra's disappearance. She was going to school in Northern Utah. George (Vahsholtz) had told me of her description and it matched

Theodore but for one point, he was wearing glasses and that was inconsistent, or so I thought. I was to interview that girl the following morning, but I had a frequent guest for breakfast join us that morning. When I went to Salt Lake, she had became a wealth of information regarding Theodore, she knew him better. Her father sat in high places in Utah's judicial system. I had gotten around the red tape to talk to her originally, and after that she called me with remembrances, and I could later call her at anytime with questions. At breakfast that morning she had told us (Blakey, Vahsholtz and I) about the glasses that Ted wore. His lawyer glasses and his "cool glasses": dark frames on the lawyer glasses and tinted lens on the "cool glasses." He would wear the lawyer glasses to the law library at night or if he went to local library, the cool glasses weren't worn all that much, just in the day time. The conversation started up when we discussed the description of given to George the night before, the tinted lenses.

It was after my interview with Brenda that I kept going over the time periods for Theodore's activity the night DaRonch was kidnapped and Debra Kent's disappearance. There had been a good deal of work on I-15. I drove the route most direct from the high school to Theodore's apartment; it didn't take long maybe fifteen minutes. DaRonch had been kidnapped and escaped, and a few minutes later Debra's abductor was at the high school and then gone, and within 15 minutes of that time Theodore was on the phone with Liz – his alibi. There wasn't enough time to dump a body – none. When I got back to Colorado I called and asked Jerry and a Bountiful detective to make the same drive at least twice. They were within a few minutes of each other, not more than 15-16 minutes, which was when I dropped my theory on Jerry that Theodore had to have had Debra or her body at the house or in the car when he made that call to Liz. They thought I was nuts.

Melissa Smith's father was the Chief of Police of Midvale, Utah, the town from which she disappeared. Jerry had forewarned me that Louie, Melissa's father, and her younger sister were very critical of the lack of investigation by the Salt Lake County Sheriff's Office. I had an appointment to meet with him and the family on a Sunday morning in an effort to reinvestigate Melissa's murder for use as a similar transaction in Colorado.

At the meeting, Melissa's sister wasn't there; Louie was very emotional but apologetic. I explained my problem to him. I needed to find all of her friends that knew her. I had to interview everyone I could, and I needed a place to do that. He graciously gave me use of the Midvale Police Department's interview room. Most importantly, I need Melissa's young sister's help. Many of the people I was looking for had graduated, married; time was not on my side. Louie told me to go the police department and his wife would try to call her in. (It's just age I can't recall that wonderful person's name.) That meeting with Louie and his wife was one of the most painful things I had to do in my life; I had to correct Louie's incorrect belief that I had Theodore's fingerprint at the scene. That belief had been developed by misinformation from a close law enforcement friend of Louie's who knew better.

Melissa's younger sister came to the police department to speak with me. She had been very hurt by the lack of active investigation, she was very vocal and emotional, but I listened. I told her what my problems were, that I could not do what I had to do in such a short period of time and the only person I could turn to was her. If she didn't want to help me, then that would bring to stop the only investigation taking place into her sister's murder. She agreed in about that many words. I had a list of names and persons who saw Melissa the night she disappeared and others who called in that weren't interviewed. She took my list and left. About twenty minutes later she came back to the office with a couple, I interview them one at a time and as I finished the second interview I stepped out into the waiting room there were a few more people, usually couples, waiting for me. I conducted the third interview and stepped out of the interview and there were no less than 12 people out there. I started the next interview, concluding I came out of the interview room there about 24 people waiting for me. I called Vahsholtz and told him I'd be late getting back to the hotel...I finished talking to each and everyone who waited, and they all did, no one left without talking to me. What civic dedication those people had to finding Melissa's murderer. It was nearly going on 9:30. I was exhausted.

Collectively we found people who saw Melissa Smith hitchhiking up the street toward the restaurant where she was last seen. A couple of jealous girls (she was striking) noted seeing her and she talked with one of the boys in a group and he left, others saw this man sitting directly behind Melissa at the next table. We learned about their efforts to get the police to look at something other than a missing person, a run-a-way girl. Other young people who frequented the restaurant confirmed that she had been sitting alone from time to time; youngster would drop in say hello and sit for a few minutes and leave. We also learned that she left alone by the side door, as did the man that sat behind her.

Not only were Mike's Utah investigations uncovering

THE TRAIL OF TED BUNDY

new information through these interviews, but he also was able (with Jerry Thompson's permission) to transport Ted Bundy's VW to the Colorado Bureau of Investigation for the additional testing that recovered pubic hair of some of his victims that hadn't been discovered during the Utah investigation. Some of the hair from Carol DaRonch's head, also missed by Utah, came to light as well. The discovery of additional evidence was good news for investigators across the board. It meant the noose was tightening around Bundy and the momentum was now with the authorities.

Mike Fisher, who'd been working tirelessly building a case against Ted Bundy, had no illusions who and what Bundy was. He was a cold-blooded killer, a ruthless individual, and one that had to be watched at all cost. In Fisher's mind (and all the investigators felt the same way), Bundy was a dangerous predator and despite the pleasant façade the killer offered to the world, to let your guard down meant people would die. But, as Fisher would soon realize, transferring such wisdom to others would not always be successful.

When Bundy was hand-delivered by Mike Fisher and three other officers to the jailers at the Pitkin County Courthouse in Aspen in late January 1977, Fisher warned them about what kind of man Bundy was, why he was going on trial in Aspen, and the many murders he was suspected of committing. One would think that bells and whistles would have gone off immediately for those hearing these dire warnings, and extra precaution would have been taken when dealing with Bundy, but that was apparently not the case.

Bundy, for his part, did what he always had done when he encountered humans he wanted to influence: He poured on the charm. And it wasn't long before people there began to trust Ted Bundy, and many considered him nice, with a good personality, and this is what Bundy was looking for. Because Bundy was involved in assisting in his own defense, he was allowed to appear in court without leg irons and hand restraints--and this included his trips to the law library on the second floor of the building. Bundy understood this trust that had been granted him by those responsible for keeping him jailed might just be enough to allow him to execute a successful escape. This is what he counted on, and he wouldn't be disappointed. The warnings of Mike Fisher, Jerry Thompson and others wouldn't matter at all.

Before the summer of 2015, I had never seen the Aspen courthouse (Bundy's first escape site) other than in photographs. Today, because of a large tree that was planted after Bundy's time there, the far left top floor window is practically obscured from sight unless you're at the midpoint or to the right of the front of the building. Staring up at the infamous window from the sidewalk and gauging the drop, it does appear a little intimidating. But nothing is more daunting than going up to the second floor of the old courthouse and peering *out* of that window. Although it's certain Bundy let himself off that ledge as carefully as possible, it was sheer luck he didn't break a leg in that fall. He did sustain an injury, but it wasn't one that kept him from sprinting away rather quickly.

Although the room is now a courtroom, the walls still hold book shelves stacked with law books, some of which look quite old. On the day of our visit, we had to wait close to an hour until a trial concluded before we were allowed to enter and photograph Bundy's portal to freedom. This was Bundy's first escape in Colorado--and he soon would be recaptured--but it would not be his last.

After Bundy's capture, he was transferred to the Garfield County Jail in Glenwood Springs, Colorado. The jail itself was rural and unaccustomed to holding such a prisoner as Theodore Bundy. But things would not be as easy going for Bundy here as it was in Aspen. Here, their prisoner would remain shackled–hands and feet–so as to prevent another escape. Or so they believed.

Chuck Erickson, chief probation and parole officer at the jail, had an office on the second floor. During a telephone conversation on November 7, 2015, he explained how the guards would bring Bundy by elevator to the second floor so that he could use the law library, and there was no mistaking the sound of shuffling leg irons. When the sound of the jangling began, everyone knew Ted Bundy was coming down the hall. From where his office was located, Erickson said he could hear Bundy approaching but couldn't see him as he passed the open door. His secretary, Sandra Yates (a pseudonym), would hear the rattling of the chains as well, and for her, it was a sound she could do without. She didn't like seeing Bundy and she always avoided, she said, looking directly into his eyes.

Erickson, who spoke with Bundy probably a half-dozen times as he passed his cell, said the prisoner was always nice and polite, and the probation and parole officer mentioned he'd loaned Bundy a "criminal justice" type board game, because the prisoner had complained of boredom. But the game, Erickson said with a laugh, was always placing Bundy back in jail! Bundy, however, was more than just about board games, and even after his disastrous first attempt at freedom, he was determined to do it again. After he rested and regained his strength, he would again find a way to escape.

Sandra Yates has her own memories of the killer as well, although her interactions with him were infrequent. And while she acknowledged that Bundy possessed a friendly personality, she still found him to be very creepy, and she absolutely believed him to be the killer of women the investigators believed him to be. As such, she found herself on guard whenever Bundy was around.

In a December 3, 2015, telephone conversation with the

author, Yates talked of walking to the copier down the hall
and finding the shackled Bundy making copies in preparation
for court. Bundy, seeing Sandra standing there patiently
waiting, asked if she'd like to use the copier, to which she
responded, yes, but after he was finished. Bundy, ever the
polite one when interacting with people he wasn't planning
to kill, stopped immediately and allowed her to make her
copies. Once finished, Sandra left as quickly as possible and
headed back to her office.

When Bundy finally made his escape, it was under the
cover of darkness on Friday, December 30, 1977. It was the
perfect time for him to flee, as it would be New Year's Eve day
in just a matter of hours and folks in Glenwood Springs were
thinking of celebration and not the escape of America's most
notorious prisoner. Bundy, for his part, had feigned illness,
and the jailers expected him to be curled in bed, and it would
be seventeen hours before they first became suspicious and
found the stacked books and materials shaped into the form
of a human body under the blanket. And while the escape
would be a rude awakening for the jailers, it was a sentence
of death for three individuals in Florida. Sandra Yates said
that after Bundy escaped, the police were stopping cars in
and around Glenwood Springs for several days. Of course,
their prisoner by then was long gone.

One would think that the Colorado authorities, having
had Ted Bundy slip out of their hands once, would have
taken all measures available to them to keep him securely
locked down, but this was not the case. Indeed, those at the
Garfield jail responsible for Bundy not only had knowledge
of the embarrassing first escape, but Mike Fisher had sternly
warned them of Bundy's intentions to get away again and
what the results would be if he were successful: the murder
of more women. Even more astounding was the cell in which
Bundy had been placed.

So what was the problem that led to this homicidal fiasco?

When Bundy was first brought to the Garfield County Jail, he was assigned a cell where the rather large ceiling light fixture was loose. An order had been put in to weld it shut, but the welding never occurred. I suppose it didn't make any difference to the officials running the jail, as the cell and fixture had been inspected and they apparently didn't see any way Bundy could get out through it and move about in the spaces between floors, and wherever those spaces might lead. (Remember what Bundy told his Larry Anderson about his plan of making his way through the vents of the Utah State Prison?)

Even more shockingly, jail officials soon began hearing *from other inmates* that Bundy was crawling above them at night, and they knew he was planning to escape. At this point, one would have to think that the authorities would do *something* to prevent an escape, but they didn't. Bundy would make good on his nocturnal overhead explorations and escape through a vent that led down to a jailer's apartment, after the jailer and his wife had left the building. This egregious lack of security regarding Ted Bundy would mean other women would die, and Mike Fisher's greatest concern should Bundy escape was now going to happen. Here's how Mike remembered it:

On December 31, the day of his escape from the Garfield County Jail at Glenwood Springs. My wife Dee and I had gone to the gym together that morning, we missed any report of the escape, because it was discovered while we were at the gym. When we left sometime around mid-day I stopped at my Aspen office and checked messages and then we walked out of the office. It was clearing after a big storm. The Sheriff was walking towards the court house as we walked to our car in the parking lot behind the court house. I should have known right then that something was up, he never came to the office if at all possible. As we passed we just made a casual acknowledgement of each other. Dee and I drove home and a very short time later Dick called me at the house and told me of the escape. I wasn't a happy camper. I expressed disbelief and that went to rage. My poor wife had to listen to me. I couldn't believe that he waited for me to get 20 miles away from him before he told me of the escape. I lost about 40 minutes in making my calls then calling Blakey. We knew we had a problem with the caliber of jailing staff in Garfield County. But the Sheriff of Pitkin County should have over seen his security as the move down there was to accommodate a federal restriction on Pitkin County's jail. But they didn't. Livid is a word that comes to mind in thinking of how I felt. Not only did I have to handle the investigation of Bundy's murders I had to investigate and present both escapes for prosecution, and those never were charged. We lost jurisdiction when Florida threw the switch. ... Just writing this conjures up some long held anger over that second escape. I knew if ever got out of confinement he'd kill again. I wasn't wrong! The investigation was my responsibility. His detention was the responsibility of the Pitkin County Sheriff. But in the public eye -- I was the one they waved their fingers at for his escape...

A final note on the killing that brought Mike Fisher into the case, the murder of Caryn Campbell: Working with him during the writing of *The Bundy Murders*, Mike gave me new and never before published information that I used in the book about the case of Julie Cunningham, a twenty-six-year-old woman who vanished from Vail, Colorado, on March 16, 1975, and whom Bundy later confessed to killing. (I in fact received new and previously unpublished information about four of the Bundy murders from various sources.) Mike also provided me with accurate information on the murder of Caryn Campbell.

What follows are Mike Fisher's comments concerning Caryn's disappearance and the people who saw her only moments before she disappeared. To protect the privacy of the couple who both knew Caryn and saw her only moments before she encountered Bundy, I will not include their names:

They (the couple) were personal friends of Ray [Godowski] and Caryn's, they were from Detroit, and she worked with Caryn in the hospital. Caryn had talked to his wife (girlfriend at the time) about going to get a book and Caryn was very tired, she had the key to her room in her hand. They didn't see anyone on the landing. Caryn was the last person to get on the elevator, so when the door opened, no one had to step out for her to walk out. The landing was only partially visible, remember the fog from the pool I told you about she could see Caryn for only about 10-15 yards as she walked away. We interviewed the Detroit couple before they left and when we went back to Detroit after finding Caryn's body. They were very detailed and helped with the identification of others they knew who were in the elevator and going to the function. I was establishing a schematic in my mind of who was where, and when. There was conference social thing going on that night many who knew Caryn and Ray attended while other did not. So I could actually know who was where and their approximate time that was significant -- especially when it came down to figuring out how she was taken from the building. Those people sometimes were able to tell me who they saw and where, what direction they were traveling in, did they talk, where were they going, so I was able to developed further leads for interviews, and literally find a fence of witness that surrounded Caryn's last moment. Theodore never mentioned seeing anyone. He was very short and curt at my later portion of the interviews.

Of the actual murder of Caryn Campbell, Bundy told Mike the following:

"Took her like I took the other one (Julie) I took her from the hotel after she got out of the elevator…" *"I took her to where you found her, and everything happened there…" He was referring to the Owl Creek Road. Questioning Theodore asking him for details was not getting me the icing I wanted on my cake…he was general.*

I asked him how he killed her, and he responded "Just like the others…" I had to ask him again how many times had he struck her, and he replied "Just once, I did my thing right there in the car…" While picking for details of area, he told me "….it was a snowy road; very slick I took her over the bank to where I guess you found her…" I asked if he knew if she was alive when he "put her where I found her," he looked at me like I had asked him to pass the sugar and said. "I don't know." Total indifference, he was through with her.

I asked him if had kept anything of Caryn's his first reply was no, then I asked him what he did with her clothing, "… I took her clothes, and put them in a dumpster somewhere down the valley…" (Probably near Basalt, El Jebel, or Glenwood Springs, CO.) I asked Theodore if he had kept the room key to her room (210), he just looked at me for a while, and then looked down at the table, rubbing his eyes. He did not answer for a few seconds and then told me that he didn't remember. He had kept the key.

When Mike Fisher interviewed Bundy then, at the end, he was accompanied by Matt Lindvall, the Vail, Colorado, investigator working the Cunningham case. Here's Fisher's recollection of that meeting:

My day came when I walked into the visiting area of the State Prison at Stark, Florida. Matt Lindvall, a detective from Vail, Colorado, had been assigned to me to go to Stark, Florida. Matt and I had agreed to stick together during the interviews–do them together. The long visiting room was empty, except for Theodore and his female attorney. Theodore was seated when we came in, and Matt was in front of me, the space was narrow for visitors.

Theodore listened to Matt's introduction, and he looked to the right and when he saw me, he stopped smiling and pulled at his beard, and said, "Hi, Mike." Now in this setting where Theodore desperately needed me and every other detective on his side he called me by my first name. I wasn't the impersonalized "investigator from Colorado," or the ill equipped, dummy he had tried to portray to the public, now I was Mike. Matt explained that we were there together for the Julie Cunningham murder, and Theodore wasn't happy with that, he wanted me out of the interview, but Matt didn't have the knowledge of the case, it was all in my memory and I had gathered the evidence, so Theodore was stuck. He would have talk about Colorado cases in front of me. The man he had decried as incapable, ill suited, the same man he had given that damning statement to in the Utah County jail wherein he denied killing anyone in Colorado, was now going to hear the truth and Theodore was going to tell it–it was a bittersweet setting for the two of us.

Our conversations first were directed toward what we might be able to do for him in exchange for information that would, at last, give peace to the families. I interrupted and sternly told Theodore and his lawyer that I would not allow the families of the victims or their emotions to be held hostages, and I was willing to walk away for our session and lay his request in front of the news media; I was going to pull the curtain open and expose him for the selfish manipulator that he was. Theodore stammered and reassured me that he was going to deliver, but couldn't we think in terms of the benefits if he was kept alive to aid in future study of his malady. I responded as did Matt that we were not going to attempt to intervene in the sentence of the court. You could see the fear and frustration in Theodore's facial expression, he continually stroked and pulled at his beard, he was doing just that when he turned to me and said, "Mike, this is serious, these damned people down here are serious, they're going to kill me if I don't get this stopped." I told him "that was the verdict of the court Theodore, you had other alternatives, and I will not interfere with the verdict that came from the bar of the court." If looks could kill, Theodore's would have fried me on the spot. He wasn't as bound now to giving up everything. He wanted to back out, he told Matt and I that he could not do all this without some benefit for himself.

Theodore told me that he had already talked to another investigator with the State Attorney General's Office, about debriefing the Campbell case to him and alluded to the fact that that might happen, at least was acceptable to talking on his behalf to the Governor of the State of Colorado for clemency. As Theodore put it, he "wasn't asking not be punished, I'm talking about establishing a permanent place for people like me, we can be studied, and be of assistance to people like you."

The same old Theodore, he was trying to take control of the entire situation and dictate the outcome. No more!

Of course, had the Colorado authorities been able to keep Bundy under lock and key, Fisher and Lindvall wouldn't have had to travel to Florida to hear this end-of-life confession. Indeed, had Bundy not escaped from his captors in Colorado, he may well have been found not guilty and returned to the Utah State Prison to finish his sentence of one to fifteen years for the kidnapping of Carol DaRonch. But he would never see Utah again, nor would he return to Washington State, or any place he was familiar with or once called home. He may not have known it yet, but the place where he was ultimately heading was the end of the road.

CHAPTER FIVE
The Road to the End

As previously mentioned, the inmates at the Garfield County Jail had repeatedly warned the staff that Ted Bundy was moving above them at night, saying they knew he was planning to escape. And since all the prisoners knew Bundy was getting up through the loose light fixture the jail planned to repair, and were informing the jailers, it's inconceivable that Bundy would ever have been able to continue and make good on his plans, but this is exactly what he did. Ted had won them over again.

Unlike in his first escape, Bundy would make it this time and there would be no stopping him. Going up and through the loose light fixture on that late December night in 1977, Bundy crawled to a jailer's apartment. Letting himself down into this room, he changed clothes and in moments was out and into the snowy night. After stealing a car that quickly broke down, he hitched a ride with a soldier to Denver, and caught a flight to Chicago. From there he took an Amtrak train to Ann Arbor, Michigan, where he remained for the next couple of days. While there, he went to the university library and searched for schools on the Gulf Coast (the killer was always drawn to the university setting!). Because he couldn't find one on the oceanfront, he picked Florida State University in Tallahassee as his destination.

When Bundy escaped he had at least $700 with him,

money contributed by friends for his defense fund. But after the plane ticket to Chicago, the train ticket to Ann Arbor, and the Trailways bus he took from Atlanta to Tallahassee (plus food and other expenses), he only had roughly $160 remaining. Though Bundy was low on funds, he was still able to secure a room at 409 W. College Ave., very close to the university. The house was a stately old-style Southern mansion, white, with two columns, and a beautiful, massive oak tree in the yard. Indeed, emblazoned above the front door of the house were the words "The Oak." Bundy was now within walking distance to the murders he'd commit at the Chi Omega sorority house. Margaret Bowman and Lisa Levy had less than two weeks to live.

When my wife and I arrived for a visit to Tallahassee in 2008, just prior to my completing *The Bundy Murders*, I knew The Oak was no longer standing. The house experienced a fire a number of years earlier and the structure had been torn down, and a fence surrounding the property silently tells visitors to "keep out." The massive oak tree remains (it looks like something out of a Tim Burton movie), and on the day we were there, I stood at the spot where the fence crosses the walkway leading up to the front door. Strangely, as I looked down, I noticed about three feet ahead of me a snake skin on the walkway, and it appeared to be angling towards the front door. As I stood there contemplating this, I couldn't help but think of Bundy's arrival at The Oak, and how much that snake and he had in common.

From the moment he escaped in Colorado until he arrived in Tallahassee, he was interested only in getting away from his captors. During this time the desire to kill young women would have to wait. But the need was starting to grow within Bundy again as he adjusted to life in his new home. And within two weeks of being in Florida, Ted Bundy would once again begin hunting victims.

Bundy was in easy walking distance (one-half mile) from his rooming house at 409 W. College Ave. to the Chi Omega sorority house at 661 W. Jefferson St. Next to Chi Omega was the nightclub Sherrod's, and it would be here on the night of January 14, 1978, that women would notice a weird guy who needed to be avoided (for a much fuller treatment of this night, the murders at Chi Omega, and the killing of Kimberly Leach, see my book, *The Bundy Murders*).

Unlike in Washington and Utah, where women found him handsome, attractive, and always inviting, the women at Sherrod's observed an odd man. He was described by one young woman as having a "greasy looking appearance." He was no longer the refined killer of 1974-1975. Bundy, unable to convince conscious women to leave with him, now decided to attack the unconscious women next door who were fast asleep in the Chi Omega house. That attack came during the early morning hours of January 15.

*Chi Omega sisters, Margaret Bowman and Lisa Levy,
died during Bundy's nocturnal homicidal rampage of their
sorority house (courtesy King County Archives)*

Bundy would silently creep into the house through an unlocked door. And unlike the well-planned murders before in the Pacific Northwest, here the killing would be little more than an animalistic frenzy. There would be no Lynda Ann Healy repeat; he had no desire to take anyone away from this house. Holding a thin log retrieved from a nearby stack, Bundy crept silently through the first floor, ascended the steps and began entering bedrooms where he would severely beat and otherwise assault four women that night, two of whom—Margaret Bowman and Lisa Levy—would die.

EMTs Gary Mathews and Charles Norvell arrived in the ambulance called to the Chi Omega house. Met by a sea of cops and distraught coeds, they were quickly ushered upstairs. As they reached the top of the steps, Mathews broke off from Norvell and entered one of the bedrooms, where he found Kathy Kleiner and Karen Chandler.

The light was on, and he saw immediately that both women were bloody and in a daze. There was blood on their faces, heads and on the bed. What Gary Mathews couldn't see as he worked on the women and prepared them for transport to the hospital, were three of Kleiner's teeth that were left on the bed. Both women also had broken jaws.

The night of mayhem was not over yet for Mathews and Norvell. After making the run to Chi Omega and the hospital, they drove with lights and siren blaring to an apartment at 431-A Dunwoody, the duplex home of Cheryl Thomas. The home, only four blocks from the Chi Omega house, was Bundy's second attack site of the evening.

Thankfully, Bundy was not able to kill Thomas, after the intervention of her neighbor in the duplex, Debbie Ciccarelli. Ciccarelli heard strange noises coming from next door (Cheryl crying and someone walking around) and kept calling out to Thomas through the wall, calling her phone and pounding on the wall. Bundy, who had beaten Cheryl about the head with the log, and was planning to rape and kill her, changed his mind because of all the commotion coming from next door, and quickly relieved himself instead through masturbation. Bundy then left through the same window he'd entered.

As Mathews and his partner entered Cheryl Thomas' apartment, they could see how badly she'd been beaten. What they couldn't see was that, like Karen Chandler and Kathy Kleiner, Thomas' jaw was also broken. The same log that Bundy had kept with him after he left Chi Omega, and which he used to attack Thomas, was found lying on the bedroom floor.

In an extremely odd twist, Gary Mathews would, in the near future, have an opportunity to meet the author of this destruction when Bundy, acting in concert with his defense teams, required him to sit across a table from the killer for a deposition. It is believed that Bundy, psychopath that he was, enjoyed such times, as he could hear the gory details from those who were called to respond to his crime scenes. He got a kick out of it. And, he would on occasion do the same thing while cross-examining a witness during the trial. For those who witnessed these things, and believed Bundy was guilty, it must have been extremely difficult to sit through.

When I asked Mathews about Bundy's demeanor, he said he was very polite. Of course, this was classic Bundy when he wasn't engaged in murdering someone. Mathews also mentioned that as Ted questioned him about his activities that night, he kept thinking as he looked at Bundy: "Why Chi Omega? ...Why Dunwoody?" But these questions he kept to himself.

When my wife and I visited the Chi Omega house in Tallahassee in 2008, as I was finishing up *The Bundy Murders*, I was aware that in the years since the attack, the outside of the building had been changed significantly and, quite probably, additional changes made to the building's interior, not so much as to structure but cosmetically. As we made our way to the rear of Chi Omega it became clear that the place was being gutted for extensive remodeling. I took several pictures of baseboards, doors, and other materials removed and stacked to be hauled away. And as I examined the doors, they appeared to be classic 1970s design, and my first thought was that perhaps these were doors Bundy opened as he went from room to room.

Unlike the sorority, the Dunwoody duplex where Cheryl Thomas was attacked is now long gone.

Finally satiated after the Chi Omega and Dunwoody attacks, Bundy returned to his rooming house, and those who spoke to him after his return would later tell authorities how oddly he was acting. Not only did Bundy fail to respond normally to those who greeted him, but two of the residents said they saw "Chris" (the name Bundy was using) standing on the front porch, staring blankly towards the university.

But Bundy's reign of terror in the Sunshine State was not yet over. After a brief respite, the killer would travel to Jacksonville on Monday, February 6, to kill more women but would fail to find his prey. Indeed, obtaining a victim was becoming harder and harder for Ted Bundy. But on Thursday, February 9, the killer would succeed one last time.

As he left the Holiday Inn in Lake City, Florida, that morning (Bundy liked Holiday Inns), he came upon Lake City Junior High. Merely by chance, a terrible fluke of timing allowed Bundy to see little Kimberly Diane Leach walking towards the rear door of the school, having just left a smaller detached building where she'd had a class earlier that morning. The twelve-year-old had walked out at that moment to retrieve her purse.

Bundy, who'd been circling the school in a stolen white

media van belonging to Florida State University, wasted no time in stopping the van (blocking traffic) and running up to the little girl. We don't know what he said to her, but a witness did watch as Bundy led her to the van and placed her in the passenger seat. Young Kimberly Leach would die shortly thereafter. Bundy returned to Tallahassee after the murder and dumped the van.

Today, Lake City looks very much the same as when the Kimberly Leach abduction and murder took place. The Holiday Inn where Bundy stayed, just down the road from the school, has been torn down, and Lake City Junior High is now the home of the Columbia County School Board. I only spoke to one person about the case while I was there (I was asking directions), but as soon as I mentioned Kimberly Leach, the school and my research, a frown spread across the man's face and he pointed me in the direction I needed to go. A lifelong resident of Lake City, he said he remembered the case well, and he mentioned how devastated the community was after the murder.

Bundy's life of unrelenting murder would come to an end in Pensacola, Florida, after he was arrested in the early morning hours of February 15, 1978.

Although it was the end of the killing, it was not yet the end of him. There would be two trials, the first was for the murders of the two Chi Omega members, Margaret Bowman and Lisa Levy, and the last trial was for the murder of twelve-year-old Kimberly Leach--and it would be the murder of this child that would put him in the electric chair. While there would be the seemingly endless appeals, his date with the Grim Reaper would finally arrive eleven years after his final arrest.

And the world is still trying to find out what made this particular killer tick.

CHAPTER SIX
Oddities and Insights

With this companion volume, I have, as with the first book, provided the reader with new and significant information about the case from Bundy's former friends, information that has been hidden for years. I have also trekked to the Bundy sites anew and have provided a literary and visual picture of what these locations look like today, and the "feel" of the locations as I've encountered them.

What follows are the oddities and insights that are a part of the case, not just what I learned this time around, but also those that I discovered in the records and interviews the first time I dug in my heels to find the real and complete story of the Ted Bundy murder. And while there were valid reasons to leave some of this information out of *The Bundy Murders*, there are now valid reasons to place them here.

One of the strangest oddities and encounters I had while researching the murders for my first Bundy book was the ongoing thought among Seattle investigators that Ted Bundy might be gay. It was a theme repeated in the record for a while, at least, and then it suddenly drops off. In my view, the notion has no basis in fact and nothing to substantiate it. Plainly, it was a strange supposition. And with this in mind, let's examine the trail the Washington detectives walked down, at least for a brief time.

When interviewed by investigators, two employees of the Department of Emergency Services in Olympia, Washington, gave similar stories of Bundy and what they believed his sexual orientation to be. According to a report dated October 30, 1975, one individual, a retired policeman working at the DES, said in no uncertain terms "he is thoroughly convinced that Bundy is the one we want. He suspects that Bundy is gay, *but has no facts to substantiate his suspicion* [italics are mine]." He also said that "Bundy often asked him questions about police investigations, how they were conducted, and how police go about their investigations. He is sure Bundy was deliberately pumping him." He was correct about Bundy's inquisitive nature.

Another co-worker "advises he and Bundy used to talk quite often. He believes that Bundy is gay. *Has no facts to confirm his suspicion* [italics are mine)]." He also added that "Bundy talked with him on such matters as the death penalty for capital crimes"

Other references to Bundy being gay made during the investigation are as follows:

An October 7, 1975, report details the comments of a Marleigh Lang, apparently a roommate of Bundy's San Francisco girlfriend, Carla Browning (so identified in *The Bundy Murders*) when they were attending the University of Washington. Marleigh saw Bundy as a user, interested only in Carla's money. She went so far as to say that "Bundy didn't have a car and Diane had to drive him around everywhere." She also quickly added that Carla "was out of Bundy's league." Marleigh told investigators she didn't like Bundy, and that "she got the impression that Bundy was effeminate and spoke with some sort of accent not identifiable as Washingtonian."

Marleigh Lang's comment concerning Bundy's often fluctuating accent has been echoed by many others, and

I included a number of these in *The Bundy Murders*. One comment I didn't add in that book, I'll add here because it's appropriate to the subject matter: One of the younger witnesses at Lake Sammamish who encountered Bundy, and spoke of this odd accent, went so far as to say that he sounded like a "fag."

An interesting end note from the record of Marleigh Lang has to do with her reaction after the news of the Lake Sammamish abductions exploded on the scene. Detective Roger Dunn noted in his report that "As soon as the news of Lake Sammamish broke, Marleigh thought that the suspect could be Bundy even before the composite was published."

As the homicide investigators began walking down the dead-end road of whether Ted Bundy was or was not gay, they walked back into Bundy's life from high school:

During October 1975, detectives visited Wilson High School in Tacoma, from which Bundy had graduated in 1965. They were gathering evidence from every direction possible, and this included any pertinent information from the records, as well as interviewing Bundy's teachers still employed by the school. Some teachers didn't remember him at all (and this included one who gave Bundy a final grade of "A"). They were also informed that one of Ted's former teachers had been dismissed for "homosexual activity."

While at the school, detectives interviewed one of Bundy's instructors, whom they deemed to be "very, very effeminate." The teacher, who shall remain nameless for this book, said that Bundy was "pleasant and responsive" and he saw Ted as an "original thinker." The detective penning the report ended it by saying, "I did not pry into any sexual discussions they may have had."

Investigators also contacted a doctor at the University of Washington who, they were told, would have the "best source of information for the Seattle gay community."

Another doctor at UW was questioned about Bundy's sexual proclivities, and, according to the report, responded that "there was nothing about Bundy's behavior to indicate deviant or gay inclinations," and then "spoke of how nice it would be to have Bundy or someone like him for a son-in-law."

I don't know why investigators traveled down this rabbit trail of Bundy's supposed gay lifestyle. Perhaps it began with the witness reports about his sometimes odd speech pattern, but that's just one possibility. Perhaps the Washington investigators felt emboldened when they heard that Bundy had admitted to some of his friends in Utah that he'd visited a gay bar in Salt Lake City? But even this did not mean anything, as you can't automatically assume someone who visits a gay bar is homosexual. But whatever the genesis happened to be, this trail would ultimately end without any fanfare. It simply ceased at some point in the record as if it had never been considered by the authorities.

In hindsight it seems absurd the investigators even headed down this direction, as actual male homosexual killers almost exclusively kill other males, either adults or boys (Randy Kraft, Dean Corll, Wayne Williams, Andrew Cunanan, and John Wayne Gacy to name only a few). Still, the police must have felt there was something to it or they wouldn't have been unleashing the hounds on this trail.

Judging this situation now in hindsight is easy, but at the time, not so much, as many facts about Bundy remained to be discovered. The only thing one can say for sure is that it was a wrong road to take and that it led nowhere.

One of the most important research materials I used during my writing of *The Bundy Murders*, was the Pre-Sentence Investigation Report (hereafter referred to as the P.I. Report) produced after Bundy's March 1, 1976, conviction in Utah for Carol DaRonch's abduction. From this report came many interesting insights about the killer. One aspect is the rage that shot to the surface of Bundy's personality when the probation and parole officer was interviewing him. What follows is from the report:

"It is of interest that the defendant displayed marked signs of hostility when asked about his early childhood. Specifically, when he was asked about his 'real father's whereabouts,' his face became quite contorted and reddened and he paused momentarily. He then gained composure and replied rather succinctly and [said] approximately: 'You might say that he left my mother and me and never rejoined the family.'"

Here's another example of the rage that boiled just under the surface of Bundy's outer self, this time from the files of the King County Police Department:

"On October 24, 1975, Detective Roger Dunn contacted Legal Messengers Inc. (a company Bundy worked for between May 1969 and September 1970) and interviewed Bill Chestnutt, Bundy's supervisor, who mentioned the following about Bundy's anger. 'He saw Bundy,' Detective Dunn wrote, 'get upset around work, and when he got mad about work or at someone, he would not strike out but would *clench his fists and shake and tremble with anger.*' [Italics here are mine] Apparently, rage was always with him.

"Dunn also telephoned Connie Hotelling, who was payroll clerk at Legal Messengers Inc. when Bundy was employed there. She was very impressed with Ted, and told the detective she 'would have fixed up one of her two daughters with him if he asked her.'"

Also from the P.I. Report came the testimonies of those who knew Bundy, sometimes from childhood. These are a window into those times and will be an invaluable resource to researchers who do not have access to the Utah P.I. Report.

The following information stems from an interview with Bruce Zimmer, dean of the University of Utah College of Law:

"Dean Zimmer was interviewed in his office at the University of Utah College of Law on March 4, 1976. According to Dean Zimmer, Ted Bundy did not stand out in the class. He stated that he has known Ted since approximately August 15, 1975. Dean Zimmer reported that Ted Bundy initially, during his first quarter of attendant [sic] at the University of Utah Law School, attended very poorly during his first quarter of classes. According to Dean Zimmer, Ted Bundy's main teacher was Mr. Jim Baillin, who also reported that Bundy had only attended two or three days of his class. Dean Zimmer reported that the defendant had received a few B's and all of the rest were C's. Dean Zimmer equated this with Ted's being slightly below average in his academic standing. According to Dean Zimmer, Ted Bundy behaved very responsibly after his arrest in August of 1975 in terms of informing Dean Zimmer, and also his other teachers, as to being a suspect in the kidnapping of Carol DaRonch. Ted Bundy was always viewed as rather calm in relationship to his arrests and the suspicions of kidnapping, according to Dean Zimmer, and he felt this was highly unusual because (as he indicated) he has taught at the Columbia Law School for five years prior to August 1975 and has also interviewed may [sic] suspected and convicted criminals who have always displayed some degree of agitation or fearfulness regarding possible sentencing outcome. Mr. Zimmer stated that Ted only seemed nervous once and that was when the police came to the University Of Utah College Of Law to arrest him. Dean Zimmer stated that Ted was seen two weeks prior to his being found guilty and seemed to be very calm and acted jocular and happy when he was not sure of the outcome of his sentencing two weeks away.

"Dean Zimmer stated that Ted Bundy was seen coming to Law School dressed up very fastidiously and appearing quite attractive at times but on other occasions appeared to be quite 'grubby' and 'unshaven.' Dean Zimmer stated that when Ted Bundy submitted his application for admission to the Law School that he stated that he had never been admitted to any other Law School when he had, in fact, attended the Law School at the University of Puget Sound. Dean Zimmer stated that this would be grounds for dismissal from the Law School. Dean Zimmer stated that the only unusual other thing that he could recall about Ted was that he had never signed his name on any forms or papers. He had always typed everything including his name."

The report continues:

"A collateral contact was made by way of writing from a neighbor, Mrs. Louise Storwick. She wrote a letter from Tacoma, Washington, dated March 9, 1976:

"Dear Mr. Hull:

I feel I must write to you in behalf of Theodore R. Bundy. Until Ted graduated from Wilson High School he lived one block from us. As a classmate and friend of our son, he spent many hours at our house and beach place. After Ted left Tacoma, he would come to see Mr. Storwick and me two or three times a year. We looked forward to his visits and enjoyed them very much. We were happy to have him spend any of his free time at our beach cabin. If, however, we ran into Ted at the University of Washington District, he was always open, smiling and glad to see us. We are proud of the way he applied himself to his chosen career and we even looked forward to voting for him some day.

In 1970 our three and a half year old granddaughter strayed from her parents at Green Lake in Seattle. I only wish I could impress you with a double surprise when a

*young man pulled a child from the water and it was their
daughter! And, the savior, good old Ted Bundy!*

*I know the Ted Bundy we know and admire is innocent.
I realize Ted's career has been destroyed and the bizarre
perversity has made and will continue to make his life
difficult. Please do not allow Ted to be unjustly sentenced
to unfair confinement as well.*

Sincerely,

Louise Storwick. "

Ted Bundy's sister Linda also wrote the court a letter,
dated March 12, 1976:

*"I am Ted Bundy's sister Linda. I am 23 years old
and know very well what is going on. I know my brother
and how interested and concerned he always has been
about people and he would never hurt anyone. I love my
brother very much. I believe in him when he says that he
did not [intend] to hurt that girl.*

*My brother worked very hard to get somewhere in
life. It was not easy, going to school and working to pay
his way through school. My brother wants to be a good
lawyer so that he can help people. He would never hurt
anyone. My brother is not a kidnapper I'm sure. I know
one time when he saved a little girl from drowning and
another time when a man took a lady's purse and ran
off and my brother caught him and got the lady's purse
back. My brother is a good man. I cannot understand
how you think that my brother could have kidnapped
that girl. That it was no hard found evidence that proved
beyond a shadow of a doubt that my brother did what
you said he did. I know that he did not do it.*

*Ted has always been very concerned about his family.
I can remember one time when he was home I understand
my sister [Sandra] was going out. My brother asked who*

she was going out with and where was she going because he was concerned. He has been concerned about me and my family because I live alone with my two children. Even though he was away from home and busy with work and school he always found time to call to see that everyone was alright. Ted has always been concerned about my brother, Glen as to what he was going to do when he was done with high school. I know that he has talked to my parents about getting Glen to get a job or to go into college. He is now in the Navy. Ted has always been a very special person to our little brother, Richard. We all believe in our brother and believe him when he says that he did not kidnap a girl. We know he is not guilty because we know him better than anyone else does. I love my brother very much and believe in him. My brother has lots of friends and they all believe in him, too. Thank you for taking time to read my letter. I am sure you are a good man, too.

Sincerely,

Linda J. Bundy"

The report continues:

"A collateral contact was held by way of writing with a Mrs. Nancy Aherens. The letter dated March 10, 1976, is as follows:

Dear Mr. Hull,

I have know [sic] Teddy just about all of my life, having attended First United Methodist Church. Ted and his family were always good workers in the church and usually people who grow up in the church don't stray.

Teddy was always there, eager to learn and understand the Lord's teaching. It is my prayer that each person involved in this case, from judge to you, has prayed for guidance. I hope that you, the judge and others concerned have reason beyond a doubt to convict, judge and sentence.

Ted is not the person who does this sort of thing! I feel as though I know him as well as my own brother and I doubt that he is the guilty party. I thrust [sic] him now as I always have and I believe and [sic] injustice has been done.

In conclusion I can only pray God's guidance through the Holy Spirit into the hearts and minds of those persons deciding on Ted's future.

Sincerely,

Nancy Aherens (Mrs. Edward Aherens)"

What follows are two medical evaluations. The first is from Van O. Austin. M.D., prison psychiatrist. The letter is addressed to "the Honorable Stewart M. Hanson, Jr., Judge" and dated 7 June 1976:

Dear Judge Hanson,

I have completed my evaluation of Mr. Bundy whom you committed to the Divisions of Corrections for a ninety days presentence evaluation. My evaluation has consisted of multiple interviews, skull X-rays, electroencephalograms, a computerized thermographs brain scan, review of collateral information, review of current psychological test data, and discussions of the case with Drs. Howell and Carlisle. This report only intended to assist the court during the sentencing process.

The skull X-ray showed a small osteoma of the left frontal sinus. Otherwise, the skull X-rays, electroencephalograms, and brain scan were completely unremarkable. Because of these negative findings and an unremarkable medical history, I did not feel that further testing and neurological evaluation were indicated.

I do not feel that Mr. Bundy is psychotic. There is no

evidence of a major thinking, mood, or behavior disorder at this time. Although his mood is dominated by some ambivalence, a somewhat flat emotional responsiveness and lack of empathy, I do not feel they are present to the degree seen in psychosis. His thought process show good conduct with reality, good concept formation, and no evidence of delusions or hallucinations. If he had been psychotic in the past I would expect to see certain personality features at this time which are not present.

I can find no evidence of organic brain disease (problems associated with impairment of brain tissue function). He is fully oriented and has excellent recent and past memory. There is no evidence of impairment of any of his intellectual functions, impairment of his ability to use good judgment or impairment of his ability to show appropriate affect.

There is no evidence of neurotic disorder. He displays none of the anxiety or subjective discomfort seen in the diagnostic category. It is possible to propose that the current crime was the conduct of a hysterical neurosis of the dissociative type. This is not consistent with my current observations of his personality or psychological test data. A second neurotic condition which must be considered is an obsessive compulsive neurosis. This disorder is characterized by persistent intrusion of unwanted thoughts, urges, and/or actions which the individual is unable to stop without developing considerable anxiety. I can only find minimal support for this diagnosis during my interviews and in the psychological test data.

A fourth diagnostic category which must be considered is the personality disorders (character disorders). These disorders are characterized by deeply ingrained, life-long, maladaptive behavior patterns.

There is considerable evidence of past successful adaptive behavior in Mr. Bundy. He does have some features of the antisocial personality such as lack of guilt feelings, callousness, and a very pronounced tendency to compartmentalize and methodically rationalize his behavior. I feel that he has also used this compartmentalization and rationalization in a passive and obstructive manner during my interviews. It is my impression that this is due to the deep seated hostility which is evident on the psychological tests. At times he has lived a lonely, somewhat withdrawn, seclusive existence which is consistent with, but not diagnostic of, a schizoid personality.

I have reviewed his pattern of alcohol and drug abuse and do not feel that these are dominant features in his personality.

I have been unable to find data to support a diagnosis of sexual deviation.

His denial of memory for the crime is not consistent with amnesia due to a hysterical reaction, alcohol or drug intoxication, or temporal lobe epilepsy. This amnesia seems too circumscript and convenient to be real.

At this point, diagnostically I can only conclude that Mr. Bundy has no mental illness, but does have a personality structure which is dominated by passive aggressive features.

The question of treatment and disposition in this case poses some serious problems. The first consideration is that he has been found guilty. The second fact is that he adamantly denies his guilt and in fact denies that he has any personal problems of any magnitude that could lead to such a crime. I do not feel that he is a candidate for treatment at this time.

In conclusion, I feel that Mr. Bundy is either a man

who has no problems or is smart enough and clever enough to appear close to the edge of "normal." I do not feel he is a candidate for treatment at this time. Since it has been determined by the court that he is not telling the truth regarding his present crime, I seriously question if he can be expected to tell the truth regarding participation in any program or probation agreement. It is my feeling that there is much more to his personality structure than either the psychologist or I have been able to determine. However, as long as he compartmentalizes, rationalizes, and debates every facet of his life, I do not feel that I adequately know him, and until I do, I cannot preduct [sic] his future behavior.

The following report is from Dr. A.L. Carlisle, Ph.D., clinical psychologist:

Test Behavior

Mr. Bundy was moderately cooperative throughout the assessment. He was given several tests and was interviewed for over 20 hours over a six week period. He took each of the tests but often questioned their usefulness stating he felt they were too open to subjective interpretation.

At times he seemed happy and outgoing. At other times he was angry and depressed. There were also times of rapid mood changes. Overall, he was extremely guarded throughout the interview. He picked his words very carefully. He was defensive, evasive and noncommittal.

Although he showed general control in his voice and through his facial expression, he demonstrated some anxiety through deep sighing when approaching the projective tests and perspired fairly heavily at certain points during the interview, indicating the presence of anxiety.

Test and interview material were evaluated by the psychology staff at the Utah State Prison.

Intellectual Assessment

On the intelligence test, Mr. Bundy obtained an I.Q. of 122 which places him in the category of Superior intelligence. He scored high in most areas on the Education Performance Test and also scored high in most areas of the GATB. In general, his intellectual abilities are very good, as is also evidenced by his general college success. There were no indications of cerebral dysfunction found in the testing.

Personality Assessment

There were no indications of psychotic thinking or ideation found in the testing nor in the interview. He is reality oriented and can respond to the demands of most situations in an appropriate manner.

The psychological testing consisted of objective, paper-and-pencil tests and projective tests. In the former, the person basically tells how he sees himself. Mr. Bundy appeared in a very favorable light in these tests, giving an impression of a very well adjusted person with no significant problems, anxieties or other negative emotions. Mr. Bundy sees himself as a fairly open person. This contrasted with the strong defensiveness shown throughout all the interviews. He also viewed himself as a person who experiences almost no anxiety, yet he showed definite indications of anxiety at times during the interviews. In general, the scores of the objective tests portray the picture of a person who is happy, confident and well adjusted. These results contrasted with the results found in the projective tests and in the interviews. Even the turmoil he is experiencing because of his present situation did not show up on the objective tests. An intelligent person can answer the questions to place himself in a favorable light, which would help explain the conflicting results. Because of the discrepancy between the two types of tests, further testing and extended interview time was undertaken.

The following personality picture was obtained from testing and the interview data. Mr. Bundy is an intelligent person with a good verbal ability. He can present himself well and makes a good initial impression on most persons. Thus, he tends to win friends easily. He has a strong desire for achievement and has good perseverance in working toward his occupational goals. He has often withdrawn from his educational pursuits which has shown a definite pattern of instability but he does show determination in his desire to eventually reach his goal.

Mr. Bundy is a "private" person who does not allow himself to become know [sic] very intimately by others. When one tries to understand him he becomes evasive. Outwardly he appears confident and reveals himself as a secure person. Underneath this veneer are fairly strong feelings of insecurity. He has a strong need for structure and control, such as in interpersonal relationships and in control of his own emotions. In the California Life Goals Evaluation Schedules he scored very high in the area of security (to have freedom from want), and high in the area of power (to control the actions of others), Leadership (to guide others with their consent), Interesting Experiences (to desire the avoidance of boredom), Self-Expression (to desire self-fulfillment), and Independence (to live one's life in one's own way). He becomes somewhat threatened by people unless he feels he can structure the outcome of the relationship. The testing revealed an over responsiveness to his emotions which would indicate his defenses are not always adequate.

The constant theme running throughout the testing was a view of women being more competent than men. There were also indications of a fairly strong dependency on women, and yet he had a strong need to be independent I feel this creates a fairly strong conflict in that he would like a close relationship with females but is fearful of being hurt by them. There were indications of general anger and more particularly, well masked anger toward women. His attempt to remain emotionally distant from others is probably a defense against being hurt by them. There were indications of a fear of being put down and of humiliation which relates to this.

He has difficulty handling stress and has a strong tendency to run from his problems. That his defenses break down under stress is shown by his general instability, both in the past and with his inability in adjusting during his first quarter at the University of Utah. His use of marijuana and the fact that he was a heavy drinker at one time are also are indicators of difficulty handling stress. These correlate with the evidence of anxiety, loneliness, and depression found in the testing.

There were signs of incongruity and dishonesty found in the assessment. In the Fall of 1975 Mr. Bundy joined the L.D.S. Church, yet contrary to church law he maintained his smoking, drinking, smoking of marijuana and his sexual habits. This shows incongruity between his professed beliefs and his behavior, and indicates he must have been untruthful during his pre-baptism interview.

Passive-aggressive features were also evident. I feel there was a good deal of hostility directed toward me and other personnel even though he would carefully point out that it was not aimed directly at us personally.

The above personality profile is consistent with the possibility of violence and is consistent with the nature of the crime for which he is convicted. A prediction cannot be made as to whether or not Mr. Bundy will show violence in the future as the best predictor is past behavior, and he disclaims any violent acts in the past, including his present charge. However, I feel Mr. Bundy has not allowed me to get to know him and I believe there are many significant things about him that remain hidden. Therefore, I cannot comfortably say he would be a good risk if placed on probation.

The following is taken from a letter that Dr. A.L. Carlisle wrote to my late friend, Jim Massie. It does not carry a date but probably is from the 1980s. Dr. Carlisle gave me permission (Jim had already done so) to include his letter in my 2009 book, *The Bundy Murders*, and portions of this mini Ted Bundy bio are in fact used in the book. For this companion volume, however, I have decided to use nearly the entire communication as I believe it is beneficial to the understanding of Ted Bundy. It contains statements from Bundy, which Dr. Carlisle has noted through the use of quotation marks.

As a child, Ted experienced both happiness and sadness. His family was fairly poor and he compared himself to other family members who were more wealthy. He was somewhat out of place in his environment and at times he was led to believe he didn't belong. At one point in his early school career Ted lived among Italians and he would run from them, to avoid fights. He wasn't of the same religion nor race. He experienced a dividing line between himself and them. During this period of his life, he had a teacher who "put the fear of God in you."

He had a grandfather who had an intense interest in literature and science. He was a well educated person and Ted wanted to pattern his life after him. It may well be that he began at this early age to attempt to find identity through achievement. At one point, he longed to be able to achieve like some of the other children, but he couldn't, which bothered him.

While in junior high school, he ran for student president, and he lost–and it appears that while he helped others run for some office when he was in high school, he never attempted such himself. He started dating while in junior high. But for some reason he stopped and didn't date until he was in his senior year. Part of the reason may be that he didn't have a car nor did he have much money. While in junior high he became less dependent on friends and more of an individualist. He became more interested in academics and memorized things he heard on the radio. In high school, he felt somewhat left behind as his friends went in other directions.

After he graduated he went to the University of Puget Sound. He longed for a beautiful coed. But he didn't feel he had the social skills to cope with it. He had a desire to achieve and he had some fairly noble goals. When he went to the University of Washington, he wanted to major in Asian studies. He wanted to develop his knowledge and skills to the point that he could gain a position of authority and improve relations between China and the USA. However, he found that he couldn't comfortably settle on a suitable major, so this didn't work out for him.

He finally met his beautiful coed. She was well dressed, well groomed and was socially skilled. She had poise and confidence, and her family was very wealthy. She had everything that Ted wanted to balance off his lack of confidence and his lack of social skills. If he could get her to fall in love with him, it would help him to develop the powerful, competent, and respected self-image that he had always wanted. If someone so beautiful, so rich, *and so impressive could fall in love with him, it would mean that he was really the diamond in the rough that he wanted to feel he was and that she was seeing beyond the outer grain into the truly great soul that was hidden within.*

However, she saw him as "pitifully weak," as a person who would not stand up for himself, and as a person she could not respect. She broke off the relationship which hurt Ted very much. He later left the area and went back east. He again contacted her when he returned and she saw him as a totally different person. He now had self confidence, poise, was outgoing and showed power behind his personality.

During this period of time, Ted developed another relationship which he continued until he came to Utah. This was not always a smooth relationship and at one point he was deeply hurt by her. He dated other girls as well, and attempted to put them on a pedestal, only to try to pull them off again. Some women felt their relationship with him was a power struggle. He was developing definite problems by this time as indicated by the boating incident and the incident when he shoved a girl's head under the water in a river and held it there until her air was almost gone.

By the fall of 1973 two opposite personalities were seen in him, depending on the mood he was in or the amount of stress he was under. On one hand, he was outgoing, confident, verbal, had poise and was able to relate well in a salesman-like manner. On the other hand, he was angry, jealous, seemed to have a secret life that he kept hidden from others, and was engaging in some aggressive sexual practices that got out of hand.

... By this time, Ted must have become a victim to his own obsessive thoughts and fantasies. The personality of

a rapist-murderer was well developed through hundreds of hours of living and [reliving] fantasies of acts he would later be committing with all of the excitement and inherent feelings of power, control and mastery that come through such a fantasy life. While he may well have regretted the acts he committed, he found that he could not get away from the overpowering obsessions until he acted them out. This led him from one crime to the next until he was finally caught.

While probably not a true multiple personality, Ted has two sides to him. On one hand, he was very friendly, warm, and showed tender feelings. I saw him with tears in his eyes more than once, and I do not feel that this was just an attempt to make an impression on me. He needed to be loved and accepted and approved of by others. He was lonely and was dependent on women for the feelings of closeness he so needed.

On the other hand, he was distant, cold, calculating. He lived his life in a compulsive manner that was well ordered and exact. Events and actions as well as conversations were planned and rehearsed many times before they took place. It was very important for him to never be caught off his guard. Life was like a chess game to him. He was always mentally two moves ahead of his opponent, so no matter what move was made he always had several suitable countering actions that could assure him success. However, outward appearing stability was countered by inward instability. Incarceration and continuous pressure broke down his controls until he ended up where he is today.

Lastly, no "oddity" list would be complete without at least one of Bundy's legal ramblings. What follows is from the Presentence Investigation Report of June 8, 1976, and it is Bundy's response to the investigators' request for a "statement." I will not be including the entire statement, as it rambles on far longer than it should and repeats events well known pertaining to the Carol DaRonch abduction (which Bundy denies, of course). But I will present enough of Bundy's "argument' to give readers a sufficient idea of the mindset of the then-incarcerated killer.

Concerning November 8, 1974, and Bundy's arrest of August 16, 1975, Bundy has this to say:

If I cannot remember precisely what occurred on a date which is now eighteen and on-half [sic] months old and which occurred eleven months prior to my arrest for kidnapping, it is because my memory does not improve with time. It is safe to say that I was not doing, however, I was not having heart surgery, nor was I taking ballet lessons, nor was I in Mexico, nor was I abducting a complete stranger at gunpoint. There are just some things a person does not forget and just some things a person is not inclined to do under any circumstances.

The point is that my version of my whereabouts and activities on November 8, although understandably vague, have not been refuted by any testimony or physical evidence other than the testimony of carol DaRonch. The fact is that evidence tending to exculpate me was not successfully challenged or refuted. The reality is that the entirety of the defense's case was disbelieved.

But the truth was that Bundy was not believed by Judge Hanson, and that Carol DaRonch was very much believed by the judge. And in the end, this is all that mattered.

Pertaining to Bundy's murder kit, which was confiscated during his August 16 arrest, the killer wrote the following:

The fact that I was stopped on August 16, 1975, and that handcuffs were found in my car was a dominating factor in the kidnapping trial. Undeniably, handcuffs, a crowbar, ski mask, pantyhose, strips of cloth, an ice pick were collected from various locations in my car. The fact is I have never contemplated using these things for any unlawful purpose, nor can any such purpose be shown. The fact is that these items were a part of a vast array of tools and miscellania [sic] carried in my car, some as "strange" as the allegedly nefarious items seized. Not seized by the police as [sic] an Army shovel, plastic boat oars, flairs, tire chains, VW repair manuals, hacksaws, coveralls, a rubber hose, cans of oil, a length of heavy chain, and a complete tool box containing among other things, a rubber mallet.

Admittedly, the circumstances were unusual. If my explanation involving the use of marijuana and my late working hours is not to be believed, then, I suppose some will turn to a plethora of clandestine hypothesis which lack only one thing: evidence to substantiate them. So while I stand guilty of being strange on one occasion at the age of twenty-nine, I am perplexed at the imaginative insinuations which attempts to link the "strangeness" with a ten-month old kidnapping.

If Bundy was "perplexed" then, his condition would only worsen in the coming weeks and months, as pressure from Colorado investigator Mike Fisher would finally pay off when he obtained a warrant against Bundy for the murder of Caryn Campbell, setting the unfortunate stage for the killer's escape-interrupted and bloody trek to the end of the road.

CHAPTER SEVEN
Bundy: A Man of Letters

The following letters were written by Ted Bundy and mailed to the late true crime writer Ann Rule. They had been co-workers and friends in Washington, and yet, in retrospect, given what we know about Ted Bundy, was it even possible for him to truly be a friend to anybody? In any event, these letters, which are now part of the official record (as are others) are included here as they reveal interesting aspects of the mind and emotions of Bundy the man, and yes, Bundy the killer.

It is important to add that at times, as you read this correspondence, you'll notice it is dripping with melodrama, which is classic Bundy. Such excursions into the juvenile traits of this killer can be found in official documents penned by him, and occasionally in court transcripts.

Key elements of his thinking are on display too, and it's a thinking he'd employ against the investigators throughout the years. I could stop at every other sentence and add commentary, but I won't. I'll leave it up to the reader to see all the twists and turns in Bundy's mind.

The first letter bears an October 8 date and the second, October 23. Both letters were most likely written in 1976 while he was ensconced at the Utah State Prison:

Wednesday October 8
Dear Ann:
The daylight which manages to struggle through the dirt-coated, screen-covered windows outside my cell are gone. Shadows cast by countless bars, lace the walls and floors. Echoes of flushing toilets and a half a dozen televisions wash down the halls. Darkness has come again to signal the end to another day's journey into night. These are the hours when I serve my "hard time." Hours, which themselves, become days.

These are not necessarily sad reflections. They represent an attempt to understand and cope with this new environment. My world is cage. How many men before me have written these same words? How many have struggled vainly to describe the cruel, metamorphosis that occurs to one in captivity? And how many have concluded that there are no satisfactory words to communicate their feelings except to cry "My God, I want my freedom!"

The ground rules for survival change on the "inside." My cellmate, who casts himself in the role of the middle-aged, star crossed alcoholic, said it best. "Listen kid; don't give away anything. Withdraw into yourself. Save everything, you might need it later." Don't give anything away. Withdraw into yourself. Don't trust anybody; words of a veteran to the kid whet behind the ears.

Putting this advice into practice is the real education. You hide cigarettes when trustees wander by! When the cigarettes are gone you learn to roll tobacco. When the papers run out you roll with paper from a sack. Matches, being scarce, are split in half. Sugar, salt, excess food, such as oranges, and Styrofoam cups are cached. Toilet paper is treasured. The lessons continue. Prisoners invented recycling.

Your life is dependent on trustees and jailers. They are the slender and unpredictable threads to the outside and the few comforts that are provided upon request. You want a telephone call, a razor to shave with, toilet paper, another blanket, or soap. When or whether you get it at all depends on how they feel at any particular moment. You say "please" and "sir" and cross your fingers hoping your request did not fall upon deaf ears.

Then there are the treasures. The letter from a friend can warm a cold cell. At visiting time I listen for the hard mechanical click that means the door will soon open, and , then breathlessly, for my name to be called. To know that someone remembers makes me feel whole and human again.

So many observations. So many new insights. It is life stripped bare. Basic and fundamental. I have yet to fully understand it. But each day I become more accustomed to these barren surroundings. Yes, there is great pressure to draw into yourself, suspect others, become passive, horde material possessions, and, in short, sever yourself from the outside world by suppressing treasured memories of freedom. In the desert, also, many flowers bloom. So it is that in this jail. I, too, am growing and discovering new things about myself and others. There are good people here who do their best. But their best could never stop my longing for the day when I will be free.

Sometimes I have the feeling, sitting in my cell, that I am in the eye of a hurricane. Outside rage court battle [sic], investigations and press coverage spawned in the wake of my arrest. The real pain must now be endured by my friends and loved ones who are subjected to the probing, rumor, innuendo and exaggeration. Their reward and mine will come in time, although none of our lives can ever be the same again. The hurricane always leaves its mark but life does go on.

The night time hours are the hard hours. I make them easier by dwelling on the building which must be done when the storm has passed. I will be free. And someday, Ann, you and I will look upon this letter as a note from a nightmare.

Love

ted

P.S. Please share this letter with others. I cannot hope to write to every one of my friends. I want them to know.

Thursday October 23

Dear Ann:

Without a typewriter, I feel like a monk. Handwriting has always been such a painful operation when it must be legible. Being here has given me the habit. I've asked for a black robe, goose quill pens and ink.

Your thoughtful words are well taken. Don't hesitate to speak your mind. Your writing skill and sensitivity are gifts which make your letters very special to me.

My mental attitude is super healthy. I have not dwelt in bitterness. There are some hard lessons which have been learned slowly. Unknown difficulties wait ahead. I am eager to encounter them. Currently, my life is stable.

You may have heard that my preliminary hearing has been postponed to November 21, three days before my birthday. This was an important delay. It will give John time to catch up with the police and my family time to raise John's retainer.

Two things, briefly: First, personal items such as writing material and candy bars are purchased through the jail's commissary. You could send stamps, however. Next, you mentioned a great sloshy [sic] downpour that had swallowed Seattle. I can't wait to stand on some

Seattle street corner and just let the rain drench me; soak me to the skin.

I have written some verse. Not poetry but verse. It's simple and ragged. The miracles it has worked in my mind is profound. Here's one that I wrote last night. Its [sic] called "Nights of Days."

This is no way to be
Man ought to be free
That man should be me
Talk to the walls
Echoes down the halls
Dream of dreams
An allusion freedom seems
Write thoughts on paper by reams

Toilet flushes
Water gushes
Makes such a noise
Lack of privacy annoys
Nightime [sic] sounds
Jailer makes rounds
No freedom abounds
Prisoners are clowns

So the night slowly passes
No wine or wine glasses
No girls to make passes
Just us caged asses
Cards are alright
I play them all night

Sleep comes on slowly
Read the words of the wholly
The scriptures bring peace

They talk of release
They bring you to God
I'm here that seems odd
But His gift is so clear
I find that He's near
Mercy and redemption
Without an exception
He puts me at ease
Jailer, do what you please
No harm can befall me
When the Savior does call me

I look back on this day
And what can I say
More of my life wasted
No freedom I've tasted
7:30 is chow time
At that hour who feels fine
Milk, mush, and toast
Not much of to boast

Sweep the floors
Talk of whores
Hear the thunder of prison doors
Do your chores
Listen to bores
How guys made scores
Or escaped to distant shores

I wrote a letter
That made me feel better
Words to the outside
That's how I keep my pride
I write words of hope

It's really no soap
I mean what I say
Where there's hope there's a way
I'll be free some day

I sleep quite a lot
Escape though it's not
In sleep I don't care
I forget the night mare
The bars and the screams
Are not in my dreams
I don't smoke cigarettes
Or have sad regrets
This sleep liberation
Is tranquil salvation

The verses continue almost endlessly as Ted wallows in his prison life. Indeed, he just about covers all angles in his writings; including God. About midway through this long poetic stream, he even gives a hats-off to his Salt Lake City attorney, John O'Connell:

My attorney is here
Words of cheer
Build the case
After facts chase
From office to jail house race
Outside he is calm
Inside, ticks a bomb
He's really intense
And yet he makes sense
Which inspires confidence
How noble he seems
His bearded face beams
How skilled are his eyes

That search for disguise
He's hurt if his client lies
This man's a creation
A master of oration
Concerned by a client's perturbation
An immaculate legal mutation

CHAPTER EIGHT
Epilogue

Will we ever stop talking, or thinking, or reading about Theodore Bundy? No, I don't believe we will. There are just too many strange factors surrounding this particular killer of women, and it's unlikely the public will lose interest in him any time soon. He's unlike any other killer out there, past or present. When you look at the number of murders he committed (a minimum of 36, but probably many more), and the boldness of the abductions--Lynda Ann Healy, Debra Kent, and two young women at Lake Sammamish to name only a few--you have an unusual predator who stands out from the crowd. However, when you add his background to the mix--a college graduate and current (during the murders) law student who'd been a rising star in the Washington state political scene--then Bundy shoots way ahead of the pack of American serial killers.

Indeed, I predict that in the coming decades, Ted Bundy will become here in the United States what Jack the Ripper became to the United Kingdom so long ago; that is to say, I believe Bundy will be studied, contemplated and written about well into the next century and beyond. Others may fade away, but he will not.

In this book, my companion volume to *The Bundy Murders*, I have endeavored to once again record the voices of those who were involved with the Bundy murder cases, and some of these voices are being published for the first time. As a historian, I consider this of utmost importance, especially since the participants are now getting older and time waits for no one. As the importance of this began to dawn upon me, I decided right away that if I was ever going to tackle another book on the Bundy case, it should be done now, and so the journey began.

ACKNOWLEDGMENTS

The writing of any nonfiction book will, of necessity, require the help of many individuals, sometimes from the past, and always from the present. And when you're writing a book where many of the participants are getting up in years, it's especially gratifying to record their thoughts for posterity--and especially so with those involved with the strange case of the Ted Bundy murders. As I had with my first book, *The Bundy Murders: A Comprehensive History*, I thank all the investigators and participants with whom I worked and who have a space in the book.

Many of you play a returning role in this book, albeit a much smaller one. This book, *The Trail of Ted Bundy: Digging Up the Untold Stories*, is primarily devoted to those who in many instances have not told their stories before or, if they have, have never told them in great detail or the stories may never have made it into a more permanent record, such as a book. Indeed, there are recollections contained in this book from folks telling their stories for the very first time, and it contains the "back story" to some of Bundy's murders that have never before been in print.

And for all of you who worked with me, I send a big collective "Thank you!" Whether you realize it or not, you have all done a great service to generations of readers and researchers of this case, by first graciously coming forward (responding to my requests) and then traveling back in time to tell us what it was like to be closely involved with Ted Bundy.

Now, individually, I would like to thank the following people from the respective states.

Washington:

The now retired waitress (who desires to remain anonymous) who worked at the Denny's on Sixth Avenue in Tacoma, who knew Bundy as a regular and shared her feelings and remembrances with me; Mike McCann, who, from his cell phone to mine, gave me excellent directions as I crisscrossed the state, walking and photographing the various sites pertaining to Ted Bundy and his crimes; Kent Barnard, who had been visiting his girlfriend at what was then Central Washington State College (CWSC) and twice saw Bundy that evening as he trolled for a victim. Kent was very helpful to me and added information not originally contained in the official report; Dave Woody, for his excellent assistance with finding people who remained elusive to me and for the invaluable work he's done to locate the exact spot at CWSC where there was a short bridge over the man-made pond and for determining *exactly* where the now torn-down railroad trestle had been when Bundy parked near it on the night he abducted Susan Rancourt from the school. Dave went above and beyond anything I asked of him in supplying me with the information I needed, and I'm extremely grateful for all the information he sent me; Capt. Mike Luvera of Central Washington University Police, and other members in the department, who aided me in my search; Randolph Stilson, archivist at The Evergreen State College in Olympia (he started there in 1974!), who helped me discover the actual site on campus of the jazz concert that Donna Manson was heading to when she disappeared; Rebecca Pixler, assistant archivist, King County Archives; Professor Julia Stringfellow, university archivist and department chair, Central Washington University; the owners and staff of Dante's tavern in Seattle.

Oregon:

The late Lorraine Fargo, a friend of Kathy Parks (and the last person other than Bundy to speak with her), who contacted me after the publication of *The Bundy Murders* and provided me with much additional information that will be found in this book, as well confirming a couple of my theories about that night that otherwise might never have been verified. I was also happy to count her as a friend before her passing; I would also like to thank Jason Zanon, headsman of the very popular website Executed Today (no connection to Oregon), where I have been "chairing" the Ted Bundy page since January 2009 (and where we now have almost 8,000 posts). Jason has also permitted me to reproduce those portions where Lorraine Fargo kindly answered questions (original content) at Executed Today, and some of those answers are a combination of emails sent to me that Lorraine incorporated into the conversation at ET; and Steven Costa, who knew Kathy Parks when they attended the same college in their home state of California, and has allowed me to use material from a remembrance page he has posted on Facebook honoring Kathy.

Utah:

I would like to thank Carol Bartholomew (the widow of Wynn Bartholomew, who was mentioned in my first Bundy book) who, in 1975, had her picture taken with Ted Bundy as he helped her dry dishes. Carol was very gracious when I contacted her, and she provided me with the story behind that iconic photo. She also told me what it was like to know Bundy after he sought out fellowship in the Mormon Church before being exposed as a killer; I must also thank Larry Anderson and John Homer, who were also very kind to me, providing me with many interesting insights, revelations, and a heretofore unpublished look at Bundy's time with them. The information they gave me about their former friend provided exceedingly important behind-the-scenes knowledge that is of paramount importance to understanding the "back story" of Ted Bundy's time in Utah; I would also like to once again thank retired Salt Lake City Sheriff's Detective Jerry Thompson for his interactions with me the first time around as I penned *The Bundy Murders*. Jerry's help was invaluable to me then and what he provided to me almost a decade ago is helping me now as well!

Idaho:

Once again, I would like to thank Russ Reneau, retired investigator with the Idaho Attorney General's Office, who gave of his time to help me during the writing of my first book on Ted Bundy and has done so again this time around, especially so in providing clarification to correct some myths surrounding the abduction of Lynette Culver that pop up from time to time.

Colorado:

Charles Erickson, head officer for probation and parole in Glenwood Springs, whose office was housed in the jail and who had perhaps a dozen interactions with Bundy prior to his second and final escape from a jail in the state; Sandra Yates (a pseudonym), Charles Erickson's secretary, who had her own uncomfortable dealings with Bundy, and who shared with me her memories of what it was like to see and speak with Bundy while he was housed in the jail in Glenwood Springs; and retired Investigator Mike Fisher, of the Pitkin County District Attorney's Office, who aided me greatly in the writing of my first book on Ted Bundy and whose materials from that time I'm using once more, and to whom I'm grateful beyond words.

Florida:

Finally, Gary Mathews, who kindly shared his memories

of being one of the paramedics who made the run to Chi Omega after Bundy's rampage there and who also assisted Cheryl Thomas after she was attacked by Bundy less than an hour later at her Dunwoody apartment.

The author wishes to thank the McFarland Publishing Co., which published his book *The Bundy Murders*. Several quotes from that book were repeated in *The Trail of Ted Bundy*.

ABOUT THE AUTHOR

A writer of history and true crime, Kevin M. Sullivan is the author of eleven books, a former investigative journalist for both print and online media, and is a recognized authority on serial sex killer Ted Bundy. Indeed, his "break-out" book, *The Bundy Murders: A Comprehensive History*, published by McFarland in 2009, was the catalyst that brought him much attention in the true crime world, leading to numerous radio program appearances and contacts from documentarians both in the United States and the United Kingdom. Portions of this work also appear in the college textbook, *Abnormal Psychology: Clinical Perspectives on Psychological Disorders*, published by McGraw-Hill in November 2012.

Use this link to sign up for advance notice
of new books from Kevin Sullivan
http://wildbluepress.com/AdvanceNotice

Word-of-mouth is critical to an author's long-term success.
If you appreciated this book please leave a review on the
Amazon sales page:
http://wbp.bz/thetrailoftedbundyreviews

Other Books By Kevin Sullivan

**The Bundy Secrets: Hidden Files on
America's Worst Serial Killer**
wbp.bz/bundysecrets

Kentucky Bloodbath
wbp.bz/kb

VAMPIRE: The Richard Chase Murders
wbp.bz/vampire

See even more at:
http://wbp.bz/tc

More True Crime You'll Love From WildBlue Press

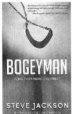

BOGEYMAN: He Was Every Parent's Nightmare by Steve Jackson
"A master class in true crime reporting. He writes with both muscle and heart." (Gregg Olsen, New York Time bestselling author). A national true crime bestseller about the efforts of tenacious Texas lawmen to solve the cold case murders of three little girls and hold their killer accountable for his horrific crimes by New York Times bestselling author Steve Jackson. *"Absorbing and haunting!"* (Ron Franscell, national bestselling author and journalist)

wbp.bz/bogeyman

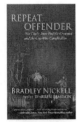

REPEAT OFFENDER by Bradley Nickell
"Best True Crime Book of 2015" (Suspense Magazine) A "Sin City" cop recounts his efforts to catch one of the most prolific criminals to ever walk the neon-lit streets of Las Vegas. *"If you like mayhem, madness, and suspense, Repeat Offender is the book to read."* (Aphrodite Jones, New York Times bestselling author)

wbp.bz/ro

DADDY'S LITTLE SECRET by Denise Wallace
"An engrossing true story." (John Ferak, bestselling author of Failure Of Justice, Body Of Proof, and Dixie's Last Stand) Daddy's Little Secret is the poignant true crime story about a daughter who, upon her father's murder, learns of his secret double-life. She had looked the other way about other hidden facets of his life - deadly secrets that could help his killer escape the death penalty, should she come forward.

wbp.bz/dls

BODY OF PROOF by John Ferak
"A superbly crafted tale of murder and mystery." – (Jim Hollock, author of award-winning BORN TO LOSE) When Jessica O'Grady, a tall, starry-eyed Omaha co-ed, disappeared in May 2006, leaving behind only a blood-stained mattress, her "Mr. Right," Christopher Edwards, became the suspect. Forensic evidence gathered by CSI stalwart Dave Kofoed, a man driven to solve high-profile murders, was used to convict Edwards. But was the evidence tainted? A true crime thriller written by bestselling author and award-winning journalist John Ferak.

wbp.bz/bop

Let Someone Else Do The Reading.
Enjoy One Of Our Audiobooks

Learn more at: http://wbp.bz/audio

Printed in Great Britain
by Amazon